Sustainable Regions

Aureus

Sustainable Regions

Making Sustainable Development work in regional economies

Edited by

Meirion Thomas
and
Martin Rhisiart

The cover material for this publication is derived from recycled material. The paper is produced from sustainable forests where trees are replanted at a higher rate than they are used.

First Published 2004

©2004 Aureus Publishing Limited

The moral rights of the authors have been asserted.

ISBN 1 899750 31 2

Printed in Great Britain.

A catalogue record for this book is available from the British Library.

Aureus Publishing Limited
Castle Court
Castle-upon-Alun
St. Bride's Major
Vale of Glamorgan
CF32 0TN

Tel: (01656) 880033 Fax: (01656) 880033
Int. tel: +44 1656 880033 Int. fax: +44 1656 880033

E-mail: info@aureus.co.uk
Web site: www.aureus.co.uk

Contents

Acknowledgement

The research presented in this book has been undertaken as part of the TASK Programme (EU Innovative Actions Programme). The authors gratefully acknowledge the financial support of the European Commission (DG Regio) and the Welsh Assembly Government.

Contributors

Caroline Cohen is a Research Associate at the ESRC Centre for Business Relationships, Accountability, Sustainability, and Society, Cardiff University

Andrew Flynn is a Senior Lecturer in Environmental Policy and Planning at Cardiff School of City and Regional Planning, and a member of the ESRC Centre for Business Relationships, Accountability, Sustainability, and Society Cardiff University

Ken Peattie is Director of the ESRC Centre for Business Relationships, Accountability, Sustainability, and Society, and Professor of Marketing and Strategy at Cardiff Business School, Cardiff University

Kevin Morgan is Director of the Regeneration Institute and Professor of European Regional Development at Cardiff School of City and Regional Planning

Adrian Morley is a Research Assistant at Cardiff School of City and Regional Planning, Cardiff University

Martin Rhisiart is Research Co-ordinator at the Observatory of Innovation, Cardiff Business School, Cardiff University

John Ryder is a Project Manager at the Small Firms Research Unit, Cardiff Business School, Cardiff University

Meirion Thomas is Director of the Observatory of Innovation, Cardiff Business School, Cardiff University

Foreword

The statutory commitment of the National Assembly for Wales to the promotion of sustainable development is a clear signal to all of us involved in Welsh society and economy that we should complement the policy intent of the National Assembly for Wales with the information, research and understanding that will allow Wales, and Welsh based institutions, to implement sustainable development effectively and efficiently.

The European Union has also set a challenge for appropriate solutions to be developed at the level of Europe's regions. Given this environment, sustainable development is now unarguably a legitimate and important area of study for academics and researchers across social, environmental and economic disciplines. On a global basis there is a substantial - and growing - interest in sustainable development. I am obviously delighted that Cardiff University has taken up this challenge and is making sustainable development a defining area of research, teaching and practice for the University.

The launch of the BRASS Research Centre by HRH the Prince of Wales in 2002 was an indication of the important role that this, an interdisciplinary research centre, holds for the University and sustainable development. BRASS combines expertise from the Business School, the Law School and the School of City and Regional Planning and allied to activities undertaken by, amongst others, the Schools of Architecture and Engineering, creates a significant critical mass of research and expertise for the University.

The publication of this book comes at an opportune moment both for Wales and for Cardiff University, and I am very pleased to be able to contribute this foreword. The Observatory of Innovation at the Cardiff Business School has developed a track record of leading-edge policy development in Wales; and, following the Wales

Regional Technology Plan and the Wales Information Society strategy, this book is another example of the ability of academic institutions to make important contributions outside its traditional teaching and research foci.

The material reported in this book is the result of the research, debate and discussion that has taken place over a two year period led by the Cardiff Business School and supported by the European Union's Innovative Actions programme. This programme, as part of a wider programme also supported by the Welsh Assembly Government, has helped to create a regional "laboratory" to test new approaches to sustainable development at the regional level. The results of the research, which are contained in this book, offer both a policy learning framework and the testing and evaluation of practical approaches to sustainable development. The research studies themselves represent a significant and original contribution to the understanding of sustainable development policy and action at the regional level.

I look forward to the healthy and informed debate that I am sure this book will engender and to Cardiff University continuing to make an important contribution to the field of sustainable development.

Dr David Grant
Vice Chancellor
Cardiff University

Chapter 1

Introduction

Meirion Thomas

Sustainable development as an objective of regional policy

Although sustainable development has a long and, some would say, a distinguished history as an objective of policy, it has taken a long time for it to take its place as an objective of regional policy. From the Limits to Growth (1972) to the first regional legislative commitment to sustainable development in the Government of Wales Act (1998), we have had almost 30 years when the concepts of sustainable development and the policy prescriptions attached to its implementation were poorly understood and debated at the regional level. However, as we move into a new century, there is growing evidence that sustainable development may be most effectively implemented at the regional level. This, despite the focus at a series of UN-led World Summits, on the big global environmental debates around global warming, population growth, water resources and biodiversity and so on.

The European Union has increasingly placed the goal of sustainable development at the heart of its policies. For example, the Amsterdam Treaty makes sustainable development one of the core tasks of the European Union. Article 2 of the EC Treaty states that

> *"The Union shall set itself the following objectives . . . to promote economic and social progress and a high level of employment and to achieve balanced and sustainable development, in particular through . . . the strengthening of economic and social cohesion".*
> (CEC, 1997)

The EU has also made the connection between economic, social and environmental policies in achieving sustainable development (Presidency Conclusions, Gothenburg European Council, June 2001). The EU sustainable development strategy focuses on ensuring that different policies reinforce one another rather than pulling in opposite directions (CEC, 2001a). It also emphasis the multi-level governance dimension of the topic and points out ways of better policy co-ordination at the Global, Union, Member States, regional and local levels.

Over the last few decades Europe has seen an increasing phenomenon of political authority and power devolution, from the central to the regional or local level. As a consequence, there has been a strengthening of regional and local autonomy and democracy. Sustainable Development and policy integration are more likely to be achieved where actual policy implementation takes place at the regional and local level (REGIONET, 2003). Therefore there is a great deal of activity in the regional and local level in achieving Sustainable Development.

The EU has explicitly supported this in its structural funds programmes requiring integrated regional strategies for sustainable development.

"The regions must find innovative solutions which guarantee sustainable development and the enhancement of regional identities – the factors which form the basis of regional, human and physical capital. The regional level is particularly appropriate for mobilising a critical mass of partners able both to promote innovation and to implement it effectively and at grass-roots level". (CEC, 2001b)

The Government of Wales Act, with its statutory commitment to sustainable development in 1998 was followed in the UK by the White Paper on Sustainable Development published by the Department of Environment Transport and the Regions (DETR, 1999). The White Paper made clear the UK Government's intention to place sustainable development on the agenda of each public body in England and followed this up with a recognition that, in establishing regional development agencies across England, the regional level

"...is the scale at which solutions (on sustainable development) can be found". (DETR, 2000).

This growing interest in sustainable development at the regional level therefore sets the scene for the TASK programme in Wales and clearly establishes sustainable development as an important area of study for academics and researchers working in the field of both sustainable development and regional policy.

The commitment of Cardiff University to study and research in the field of sustainable development is well evidenced by, for example, the BRASS Research Centre. BRASS was established by the Economic and Social Research Council in October 2001 as an interdisciplinary research centre combining expertise from the Business School, the Law School and the School of City and Regional Planning.

At the same time, regional policy researchers at the Observatory of Innovation at Cardiff Business School combined with a number of Welsh public bodies, led by the National Assembly for Wales, to propose an experimental programme of research and pilot project implementation that found support from the European Commission. The outcome of this collaboration has been the TASK Programme (Towards a Sustainable Knowledge-based region). Much of the material reported in this volume is the result of research, debate and discussion that has taken place over a two year period from January 2002 and supported under the TASK programme.

Setting the context: The TASK programme in outline

In 1996, the Cardiff Business School was heavily involved in developing the EC-funded 'Wales Regional Technology Plan' (RTP), a pathfinder for regional strategy building in Europe, which laid the groundwork to address the innovation deficit in Wales and to create a new and more consultative basis for policy making. This was closely followed by the even more ambitious Wales Information Society programme. Both of these projects can be said to have led to significant shifts in policy and associated reallocations of regional policy funding in Wales from EU, national and regional sources.

Building on these experiences, the 2-year experimental programme: "Towards a Sustainable Knowledge based Region" (TASK), funded by the National Assembly for Wales and the EU's Innovative Actions programme, has created a regional "laboratory" to test new approaches to sustainable development at the regional level. The TASK programme consisted of pilot actions in innovation, information technology and sustainable development with the aim of mainstreaming the results and policy lessons into the Objective 1 Structural Funds Programme and other strategic programmes in Wales.

Following an evaluation process devised by the National Assembly for Wales, four individual projects were chosen to complete the TASK Programme. These projects were chosen because they offered a balance between the testing of practical approaches that were related to various aspects of sustainability, with the development of a broader learning framework to allow for policy learning and development at both the strategic and operational levels:

Observatory for a Sustainable Knowledge based Region (OSKaR)

The main elements of the Observatory's programme have been research studies, best practice visits, and a consultation and dissemination programme featuring a well used and active web site (www.sustainableregions.net). The research studies, using a wide range of research groups, have investigated particular issues or areas of sustainability in considerable detail and represent a significant and original contribution in this field. In particular, the research placed a programme of best practice visits at their heart to provide first-hand knowledge of exemplary activities carried out across the EU, including Sweden, Netherlands, Spain, Scotland and Italy.

The Observatory also organised a programme of debates that reached people from all over Wales. The debates confirmed some of the main messages from the research programme and helped to clarify the views of a cross-section of Welsh society, proving to be valuable in helping to develop important lessons from the programme.

Future Technologies

The Welsh Development Agency has tested a number of 'bottom up' approaches to identify the key future technologies for Wales on a 10 year horizon. The criterion used to identify these technologies is that they should be capable of being "sustained" in Wales, that is, that they can utilise existing strengths, centres of excellence and skills without the need for constant inputs from foreign investors. The creation of long-term competencies in these technologies, and the use of the competence to generate a step change in the innovative capacity of Wales has been a key objective of the project.

LANDMAP +

The Countryside Council for Wales has tested an advanced Geographical Information System (GIS) to present the environmental, economic and social data that is essential in helping to make planning or investment decisions based on the principles of sustainability. LANDMAP was initially piloted in 1997 as an environmental decision tool using multi-layers of environmental, geological and biodiversity information. LANDMAP + has experimented by adding social and economic information onto the environmental data and then testing the outcomes on planning or land use decisions through the use of the GIS.

Sustainability, Community, Environment, Economy (SCEnE)

The SCEnE pilot action, delivered by the University of Wales, Bangor, uses a "knowledge transfer" approach that uses the University's skills base in sustainable development to assist companies and other organisations to evaluate their activities according to sustainability criteria. To improve their understanding of their sustainability performance and potential, a team of trained sustainable development 'practitioners' has worked closely with small and medium sized businesses.

The scope of sustainable development

The term "sustainable development" emerged from the debates that took place, largely during the 1970s, regarding the impact on the global environment from rapid, and seemingly endless, economic growth and the associated negative effects of population growth, environmental degradation and social changes in both the developed and developing world. Most of this debate took place at a global level beginning with the Club of Rome's report "The Limits to Growth" (Meadows et al, 1972) and continuing through a range of United Nations reports including the seminal Brundtland Commission report "Our Common Future" (WCED, 1987).

The Brundtland Commission established the 'benchmark' definition of sustainable development as:

"development that meets the needs of the present without compromising the ability of future generations to meet their own needs" (WCED, 1987)

It can be argued that linking the term "sustainable" with "development" was simply a convenient way of glossing over the tensions between the economic and ecological policy objectives of much of the world in the latter decades of the 20th century. Indeed there is a body of opinion, notably from the ecological perspective, that sees sustainable development as a 'get out' clause for governments, businesses and communities that wish to mask their real objectives of continued growth through consumption. As a result, there is still no fully accepted definition of sustainable development and no real consensus as to its implications for policy prescriptions.

The TASK projects have certainly encountered the problem that 'sustainable development' carries with it a common perception that the concept is nothing more than a convenient "canopy" under which other issues can be sheltered and developed. A "bandwagon" may be a more pejorative term. Indeed, the projects supported under the TASK Programme can, at first glance, be perceived as covering a wide range of seemingly disassociated topics – prioritising technologies and investment choices; the use of GIS; impacts on planning decisions; sustainability for businesses & communities; the development and testing of tools and a wide ranging research agenda.

However, the diversity and scope of the TASK projects and the topics that they have covered illustrate one of the most distinctive features of the sustainable development debate. Sustainable development covers social, economic and environmental aspects and implementation of sustainable development cannot be the remit of one government department, one agency or one sector of society.

The TASK projects all encountered the issue of definition albeit in different ways. The SCEnE project is certainly at the 'sharp end' of the definitional issue since it relies on working with businesses and communities to develop a strategy for achieving sustainable development. Obviously, defining what sustainable development is or may be is vital to the definition of a strategy. The WDA's Future Technologies strand has, at its heart, the notion that economic sustainability in a region may be enhanced by achieving a strong element of "self reliance" in the development and exploitation of key technologies in the future. On the face of it, this may be a long way from the LANDMAP + project that seeks to test the impact that use of a GIS may have on local planning decisions.

Whatever is the case, it is increasingly obvious from the TASK projects that accepting a broad definition of sustainable development points to a need to engage a broad range of organisations, levels of government and interest groups in the implementation of sustainability, particularly at a regional level.

For example, a community sustainable development strategy may require supportive actions from health, social services, education and economic development functions at a local, regional or even national level to be implemented. Similarly, a company sustainable development strategy may not be feasible unless coordinated action can be taken in education, training, universities or environmental services. Again, action by local, regional and national government levels may be required. Finally, if the future technologies identified by the WDA's project are to be sustainable, action may well be required in education, industry, and trade promotion to be viable.

Two common themes seem to be emerging from the experiences of the TASK projects.

Firstly the discussion regarding definitions may obscure the real point that the concept of "sustainable development" should provide an *idea of scope rather than a precise definition*. A definition is, arguably, a limiting concept and if it could be replaced by a description of the scope of "sustainable development" then a number of benefits would flow, not least in allowing connections to be made more easily between, for example, future technologies debates and local planning decisions aided by a GIS.

Secondly, the need to inspire action from a wide range of governmental as well as private and non-governmental bodies in order to implement sustainable development, may require a rethink of the relationships between traditional functional departments (horizontal governance) of local, regional, national and supra-national (EU) government as well as between the different tiers of government themselves (vertical integration). This point is discussed further by Flynn and Morgan in Chapter 2 of this book.

Public perceptions of SD

A key issue for implementing sustainable development is the extent to which the public are able and willing to engage in policy debates or to be sufficiently motivated to change their behaviour in support of a sustainable development objective. The language of sustainable development, as with the definitional question, may in itself be a barrier to public understanding and action on sustainable development.

As already noted, the TASK programme has certainly encountered difficulties in explaining sustainable development to various groups. This was reflected by the findings of a survey of over 1000 Welsh people by the Wales Consumer Council in late 2002 (Bibbings, 2003).

73% of the people surveyed were either relatively or completely unfamiliar with sustainable development with only 6% confident of being able to define sustainable development. In contrast to the Wales Consumer Council results, one of the TASK projects, SCEnE, found that 70% of the 224 people that they surveyed at the Royal Welsh Show and the Anglesey Show in July 2002 had heard of sustainable development.

Encouragingly, when the Wales Consumer Council offered people a range of definitions of sustainable development, more people picked the Brundtland definition than claimed to be familiar with sustainable development in the first place. This may be a sign that constant repetition of the definition in government papers and announcements in Wales has led the Brundtland definition to become part of general language and that it is not as arcane as many may assume. Equally, it is possible that the eminent good sense embodied in the Brundtland definition creates an 'easy pick' for people.

The survey further revealed that sustainable development is only marginally a gender issue and, despite a National Curriculum emphasis on sustainable development, amongst 16-24 year olds 81% said that they were unfamiliar with the term sustainable development. Amongst social classes, the higher social classes were much better informed and aware of sustainable development suggesting that sustainable development is still largely a professional and middle class concern.

The only conclusion that can be confidently drawn from these results is that public perceptions regarding sustainable development depends on who you ask and what you ask, a common conclusion of most surveys of perception and awareness amongst the general public. Therefore, the dangers of 'preaching to the converted' are fully evident in the area of sustainable development.

This was further reinforced during a series of 'debates' that the OSKaR project organised around Wales in the summer of 2003. Over 200 people participated in 11 debates held at venues across Wales. It was evident that many participants had differing and often conflicting views about the meaning of sustainable development. The chief obstacle to the implementation of sustainable development in Wales was regarded as being the difficulty of 'breaking habits' both amongst the public as consumers and amongst politicians and officials as policy makers. The debates revealed that many people believe that increasing awareness of sustainable development will allow explicit choices to be made and consumers to be 'empowered'. However, achieving this was felt to be impossible until people are made clearly responsible for their own actions. The comparison with the public campaign to reduce drink driving was made on more than one occasion and suggests that the public at least understand the extent of the challenge in implementing sustainable development.

The results from both surveys and debates held over recent months indicate that not only is the public imperfectly aware and informed regarding sustainable development but they also are sceptical that their leaders (politicians, civil servants and business leaders) are much better informed or 'switched on' themselves. The responses from the public, notably in the debates, also suggest that the difficulties faced by government and business in implementing sustainable development are understood. Furthermore, the challenges of dealing with multi-level governance and the pressures arising from 'juggling' both short and long term priorities make implementation of sustainable development highly problematic.

Structure of this book

So far in this introductory chapter we have been setting the scene for what now follows. We have considered the place of sustainable development in the debates regarding regional policy. This was established in both the policy and university environment that exists in Wales. The genesis and implementation of the "Towards a Sustainable Knowledge based Region" (TASK) programme have been described but not dwelt upon because at this stage of the book the issues regarding the implementation of individual projects matters less than understanding the way in which sustainable development is being defined, the way in which its scope is delineated and most importantly, the reality of the public response and awareness of sustainable development as an important topic affecting their lives.

The remaining chapters of the book set out to explore some of theses issues and, where possible, to suggest new ways of thinking about the implementation of sustainable development at the regional level in particular.

In Chapter 2, Andrew Flynn and Kevin Morgan explore the issues arising from implementing sustainable development at a regional governance level while at the same time being a 'good' citizen of the world and addressing global governance concerns and policies. There follows a series of four chapters that report on the results of research carried out as part of the TASK programme. Specifically these deal with the food sector (and local procurement in particular), the waste sector, construction and, in a slightly different vein, the place of sustainable development in the 'knowledge economy'. Each of the chapters contains descriptions and comments on other European examples of implementation of sustainable development at a regional level. These examples have been visited and studied as part of the TASK programme and form a rich vein of comparative experiences.

Following the four chapters that look in some detail at the position of sustainable development in implementation at the regional level, the view of the reader is then attracted to the horizon, with a chapter dealing with development trajectories and scenarios that Wales may face in the future of sustainable development. Based around global trends and trajectories, developed for TASK by the Finnish Futures Research Centre, the chapter brings the global back down to the regional level as experienced in Wales emphasising that a region not only exists in geographical space but also in a temporal space where the pathways are, as yet, uncertain but which sustainable development policy must try to prepare.

Finally, the strands of the book are brought together in a chapter that attempts to draw out policy lessons for implementing sustainable development at the regional level.

References

Bibbings, J. (2003) *Consumption in Wales: Encouraging the Sustainable Lifestyle*, Welsh Consumer Council

CEC (1997) *Consolidated Version of the Treaty on European Union, Common Provisions, Title I, Article 2 (ex Article B)* 97/C 240/02

CEC (2001a) Communication from the Commission, *"A Sustainable Europe for a Better World: A European Union Strategy for Sustainable Development"*, (Commission's proposal to the Gothenburg European Council) Brussels, 15.5.2001 COM (2001)264 final

CEC (2001b) Commission of the European Communities, *"The regions and the new economy : Guidelines for Innovative Actions under the ERDF in 2000-2006"*, Brussels, COM 60final

DETR (1999) Department of the Environment, Transport and the Regions, *A better quality of life. A strategy for sustainable development for the United Kingdom*

DETR (2000) Department of the Environment, Transport and the Regions, *Guidance on preparing regional sustainable development frameworks*

Meadows, D. et al (1972) *Limits to Growth* Universe Books, New York

Presidency Conclusions, Gothenburg European Council, 15 and 16 June 2001, SN 200/1/01 REV 1

REGIONET Workshop II. (2003) Rapid Report II, *Regional Sustainable Development – Strategies for Effective Multi-Level Governance*, Lillehammer/Norway, 29-31 January 2003

WCED (1987) *Our Common Future*, World Commission on Environment and Development, Oxford University Press, Oxford

Chapter 2

Governance and Sustainability

Andrew Flynn and Kevin Morgan

Introduction

Localities and regions are slowly but surely beginning to shed their Cinderella status as interlocutors in the sustainable development policy arena, and this is due almost entirely to the growing inter-dependence between subsidiarity and sustainability. That is to say the local and regional scales are coming to be recognised as vitally important arenas of sustainable development because, while sustainable development policy is largely *designed* at the national and supra-national scales, it is actually *delivered* at the sub-national scales. World summits like Rio and Johannesburg might have a useful role to play in fostering sustainable development if they raise awareness and disseminate good practice, but these global spectacles can never be a surrogate for the truly important things, like how we weave sustainable practices into the warp and weft of everyday life - into what we eat, how we travel and how we treat our waste for example. These prosaic, habitual and taken-for-granted routines will be the real measure of our collective commitment to sustainable development.

Subsidiarity is one of the most elusive of all governance concepts. By and large it is generally understood to mean the devolution of power to the lowest level which can effectively deploy it, a means of keeping power and decision-making as close to the citizen as possible. In practice, however, subsidiarity has been stymied at the top as well as at the bottom of the policy pyramid. At the upper echelons of the policy pyramid, be they in Brussels or London, subsidiarity has been compromised by the simple fact that officials and politicians are often loath to cede control to lower echelons even when central control is unable to deliver the goods. But subsidiarity has also been thwarted at the lower levels of the policy pyramid too, albeit for different reasons. At local and regional levels the main threat to subsidiarity comes from their organisational competence to handle more functions and more responsibility. In other words a combination of control and competence has rendered subsidiarity easier to preach than to practice.

Although subsidiarity might appeal to some central governments because it allows them to shed responsibility for difficult policies, the concept should really be understood to mean *sharing*, not *shedding*, responsibility in the context of a multi-level polity where the policy process (at least in the European Union) straddles supra-national, national, regional and local levels (Morgan, 2002).

As the arenas in which policy is actually implemented, localities and regions are assuming more importance because the *implementation* stage of the policy process is finally being recognised as the most important stage, even though it is the stage which has hitherto commanded the least status in the conventional policy pyramid. But it is here, 'on the ground', where the policy process must be ultimately judged a success or a failure, and it is here, at the so-called 'delivery end', that Tony Blair's governments have encountered the greatest problems.

Like many governments before them, the Blair governments have continued to extol policy design over delivery, and they have also grossly over-estimated what can be achieved by a top-down, centralised approach. The limitations of this approach were admirably summarised in a House of Commons select committee report, *Making Government Work*, which found that some of the most obdurate barriers facing public policy in the early 21st century were to be found in the very structures and conventions of government itself. Referring to the main barriers the select committee report concluded by saying that:

> 'Government in Britain is distinguished by a culture of administrative centralism, which - along with departmentalism - presents a key challenge to any sustained attempt to make the machinery of government work better. Programmes driven top-down from the centre often seem to offer the opportunity for speedy delivery, and hence fit with the imperatives for individual Ministers to be seen to make a difference to policy-making in relatively short time periods. But this approach can be at the expense of building up the local strategic capacity that will be required for durable results, and where new top-down programmes are initiated in rapid succession, and without much genuine evaluation of what is working and what is not, the results can be actively inimical to the sustained development of good public service delivery on the ground. It is essential that there is local ownership of programmes, including shared ownership of the performance measures that are used to evaluate them' (House of Commons, 2001).

Hierarchical and centralised structures, allied to silo-like departmental conventions, have proved to be a fatal combination, and perhaps this is the main reason why New Labour's public services reform programme has taken so long to deliver tangible dividends. However, these structures and conventions are beginning to be addressed, and this is why subsidiarity is becoming a central issue in UK and EU governance debates. To illustrate this point let us briefly mention three ways in which subsidiarity is assuming more importance at national and supra-national levels.

First, the growth of devolution in the UK – in Scotland, Wales, Northern Ireland and London, and to a lesser extent in the English regions too – means that the centralised, London-centric British polity is giving way, albeit slowly and modestly, to a more pluralised, multi-nodal polity in which some genuine policy experimentation is once again becoming possible for the first time since local government was effectively 'nationalised' by central government and subjected to a centralist template (Morgan and Mungham, 2000; Chaney et al, 2001). This is the constitutional context which made it possible for Wales to pursue a more robust sustainable development policy than in Whitehall, and this Welsh policy departure - known as the sustainable development scheme - constitutes the main theme of this chapter.

Second, the advent of a 'new localism' testifies to a growing recognition on the part of the Blair government that its centralised 'command and control' approach to managing the public services has failed, the clear implication being that more decision-making power needs to be devolved to the local delivery level (Corry and Stoker, 2002). On the other hand the Blair government seems ideologically averse to devolving more power to local government, not least because it doesn't trust local authorities to handle their new powers responsibly (according to central government that is). This inter-governmental conflict is part of a long standing battle between central and local government in the UK, and it reflects the fact that successive central governments in London have been profoundly uncomfortable with delegating power 'downwards' to local and regional levels, as well as 'upwards' to Brussels.

Third, subsidiarity seems set to become a more important part of the EU governance landscape, though one has to be careful here because the concept of subsidiarity has always flourished at the rhetorical level, but less so in reality. However, it does seem that we are entering a new era in the EU, not just with the shift from 15 to 25 member states, but with the growing recognition that the EU must do more to redress the 'delivery deficit' of grand policy initiatives failing to achieve much on the ground. To help to redress this problem the European Parliament's Committee on Constitutional Affairs has suggested that the principle of subsidiarity needs to be significantly enhanced – not for any grand constitutional reason interestingly enough, but for the simple reason that some 70-80% of EU programmes are managed and implemented by local and regional authorities and the latter need to be officially recognised if policy design is to be re-united with policy delivery. As regards the regions with legislative power it has been suggested that the basic treaty should recognise their role in implementing EU policy and award them the status of 'partner regions of the Union' (Lamassoure, 2002).

Our aims in this chapter are threefold: first, to examine the emergence of the sustainable development scheme under section 121 of the Government of Wales Act; second, to assess what difference it has made, if any, to the activities of the Assembly and its partners in public bodies and local government; and finally, to highlight some of the potential inter-governmental conflicts which section 121 creates for the Assembly vis-a-vis the governance levels 'above' it in London and Brussels and 'below' it in local government.

A Unique Duty: The Advent of the Sustainable Development Scheme

Under the Government of Wales Act the National Assembly for Wales assumed a responsibility for sustainable development that was unique for an elected body in the UK and, to our knowledge, also unique in the context of the EU . Section 121 of the Act requires the Assembly:

- to make a scheme setting out how it proposes, in the exercise of its functions, to promote sustainable development;
- to keep the scheme under review and in the year following each ordinary election (after the first) to consider whether it should be remade or revised;
- not to delegate the function of making, remaking or revising the scheme;
- to publish the scheme when first made and whenever subsequently remade and, if the scheme is revised without being remade, to publish the revisions or the scheme as revised (as it considers appropriate);
- to consult such persons or bodies as it considers appropriate before making, remaking or revising the scheme;
- to publish an annual report of how its proposals as set out in the scheme were implemented in that year; and
- in the year following each ordinary election, to publish a report containing an assessment of how effective its proposals (as set out in the scheme and implemented) have been in promoting sustainable development.

There are two key elements of Section 121. The first is the statutorily binding nature of the obligation and the fact that the Assembly cannot delegate this function (because the scheme has to be approved by the Assembly in plenary session). The second is the inclusive and open nature of the process of producing and maintaining the scheme.

Partnerships to promote sustainability

The responsibility placed upon the Assembly by Section 121 places considerable demands upon its delivery capacity and therefore upon its patterns of governance. The Assembly's forerunner, the Welsh Office, lacked a policy tradition and was much more focused on the delivery of programmes and services. Senior officials and politicians have not only had to reorient themselves to a new political climate but they have also had to cope with a reduced ability to draw on the policy expertise of Whitehall departments. Indeed under the Welsh Office was a political and administrative system that relied heavily on a strategic input from Whitehall and Westminster. Matters are made still more challenging because Section 121 is so novel: the Assembly could not learn from experience elsewhere in Britain or Europe but had to develop its own capacity to think through how it should mainstream sustainability within its own operations and promote it within its partners. Moreover, the emphasis on an inclusive process of preparing and maintaining the sustainable development scheme is also a novel task. Thus, the process of preparing the Sustainable Development Scheme, *Learning to Live Differently*, was characterised by genuine collaboration between a small number of Assembly Sponsored Public Bodies (ASPBs), NGOs and Assembly staff. Below we explore the development of collaborative partnership working to promote the sustainable development agenda.

The devolution agenda ushered in a more co-operative and consultative style of politics. Early on key actors showed that they wished to engage in a different style of politics and shift long-established agendas, such as refocusing the traditional economic interests that had dominated debate in Wales. Environmental or broader sustainability issues had for the most part been pushed to the policy margins but debates on devolution opened up new policy spaces into which actors with an interest in sustainability quickly moved. A good example of the shifting policy landscape surrounds the Sustainable Development Charter Group that was established to champion an alternative developmental model. The Group was a collection of over 25 environmental NGOs, key government agencies in Wales (Countryside Council for Wales, Environment Agency and Welsh Development Agency) and the Environmental Planning Research Unit at Cardiff University. It was established to debate the environmental policy implications of the devolution process and to co-ordinate attempts to lobby Parliament during the passage of the Government of Wales Bill. The Group was successful in bringing together the environmental movement in Wales with key government agencies and civil servants from the Devolution Unit within the Welsh Office who attended and contributed to several meetings held under 'Chatham House' rules. In many respects it provided a mechanism to facilitate collaboration between the different sectors of the environmental movement: from single interest NGOs to government agencies. It presaged a more collaborative form of interaction between groups and between groups and the Assembly, especially the Sustainable Development Unit (now part of the Strategic Policy Unit), that has continued (Bishop and Flynn, 1999).

Helping to secure the passage of Section 121 was a significant achievement for organisations keen to promote sustainable development in Wales. The next challenges were to continue with the more collaborative forms of working that had been established and for the Assembly to formulate its Sustainable Development Scheme (SDS) *A Sustainable Wales – Learning to Live Differently.*

The process of preparing the SDS was characterised by collaboration. The key members of the Sustainable Development Charter Group were keen to ensure that the momentum that had built up behind the inclusion of Section 121 was not lost. Following internal meetings it was agreed that the Group would approach the Assembly with an offer of assistance in the preparation of the Scheme. This agreement was reached after some debate amongst the Assembly Sponsored Public Bodies (Countryside Council for Wales (CCW), Environment Agency (Wales) and Welsh Development Agency (WDA) about whether they should attempt to involve themselves in the drafting of the scheme or wait until asked to comment or contribute. At least one Chief Executive felt that it was not the role of an ASPB role to assist in the preparation of the Scheme unless asked for specific contributions, for fear of compromising their independence and usurping the role of the civil service. The offer of assistance was accepted by the Assembly and during the course of preparing the SDS a group comprising representatives from CCW, Environment Agency, WDA, Welsh Council for Voluntary Action (WCVA) and the Department of City and Regional Planning, Cardiff University met with staff from the SDU on a regular basis to discuss the Scheme and comment on ideas and drafts. This group became known as the 'Glamorgan Group' (after the building in which it often met). It is worth noting that the Group made persistent attempts to involve representatives of the business community in the drafting of the SDS but with little success, their focus was seemingly on the emerging National Economic Development Strategy (NEDS) and arrangements for the distribution of Objective 1 funding.

The network that developed around the Glamorgan Group was largely informal and so too was its working arrangements. For those who participated in the Group it opened up access to Assembly officials and brought officials into contact with the NGO sustainable development community. The network was a bottom-up initiative and brought together those who had a common agenda to promote specific policy goals (Section 121 and the SDS) and has proved an effective means of exchanging knowledge between network participants. The Glamorgan Group operated as a sophisticated network in which its members recognised the constraints on others and in which relations of trust and respect were quickly established and these proved essential for the meaningful exchange of ideas and entering into of commitments. As we shall see the operation of the network contrasts with that between the Assembly and local government professionals dealing with sustainability. In the latter case, what might be termed a shallow network exists in which there are formal structures but only limited evidence of the transmission of knowledge.

The collaborative approach adopted in the drafting of SDS extended beyond the Glamorgan Group. Early drafts of the Scheme were posted on the Assembly's web-site in an attempt to open-up the policy-making process and engage with 'stakeholders' prior to the formal consultation period. This open process of policy making contrasts sharply with the closed system that often characterised the old Welsh Office and Whitehall. The Assembly, in plenary, formally adopted the SDS *Learning to Live Differently* in November 2000. A key theme of the SDS and the associated Action Plan is better decision making for sustainable development. The Assembly wishes both to demonstrate its commitment to the pursuit of sustainable development and to act as an exemplar to others in Wales. But has it been able to do so? Has the Assembly been able to mainstream sustainable development in its operations and that of its partners? In the following sections we briefly examine the structures and processes adopted by the Assembly to promote sustainability in its own work and that of its key partners, the ASPBs and local government. The analysis below is drawn from Flynn (2003) and involved key person interviews with staff in the Assembly, ASPBs, local government and NGOs.

Mainstreaming Sustainability in the Assembly?

The initial response of the civil service to the requirements of Section 121 was to establish a 'Sustainable Development Unit'. This mirrored the Whitehall model where a Sustainable Development Unit, with a government-wide remit to promote sustainable development, was established within the then Department of the Environment, Transport and the Regions. The Sustainable Development Unit was located within the Assembly's Environment Division of the Transport, Planning and Environment Group. Both the Units faced common challenges. First, based within a 'vertical' policy division it was not clear how they could promote the horizontal integration necessary for sustainable development across other policy divisions. Second, their location within environment departments helped perpetuate a belief amongst some policy-makers that sustainable development is an environmental issue. A more innovative model would have been to establish the Sustainable Development Unit as a horizontal unit to formulate and drive forward policy. This structural issue was 'corrected' following a debate in the Assembly chamber on the draft Sustainable Development Scheme with the Members agreeing an amendment that required the SDU to be moved to the Policy Unit.

Has the shift in the location of the SDU made much difference? The answer must be yes. First, it indicated that there was a group of politicians who had grasped more quickly than senior civil servants the organisational implications of the cross-cutting nature of sustainability. Second, the Policy Unit was strategically located and gave the SDU much better access to senior ministers than they would otherwise have experienced. Third, SDU staff were able to spend much time and effort looking outside the Assembly. As one official explained:

"We spent a lot of time working externally"

and this has undoubtedly helped to foster the generally positive views that NGOs and local government officials have of the Assembly's efforts though this is now increasingly subject to more critical comment. Subsequent reforms to the SDU have ensured that its strategic and cross-cutting approach remains as it is now part of the Strategic Policy Unit.

Nevertheless the process of learning about the implementation of sustainability has not always been easy. Key staff within the Assembly recognise that it may not always present a consistent message to the inside or outside worlds or make progress on sustainability as quickly as they should. In part, this simply reflects the limited resourcing for staff dedicated to sustainability issues. Inevitably not all topics can be covered and there has to be some 'cherry picking' in which staff identify areas where they hope that progress can be made.

Elsewhere within the Assembly there is a belief that sustainable development is being mainstreamed and that there is senior management commitment. Here two arguments are advanced. One is that many of those who are now in senior posts in the Assembly had been involved in the thinking and the debates on the Government of Wales Act. One interviewee commented:

"So at a senior official level they were well aware from the outset of the clause on sustainable development and thinking through its implications."

The second point that is made is that staff do not get appointed to senior positions unless they share the Assembly's values. Senior staff argue that therefore

"SD is more embedded than you think. …There is strategic buy-in at the highest levels to the Assembly agenda (e.g. equality)."

It is claimed that if the commitment and understanding of sustainable development were not there at senior management levels it would be spotted by the politicians.

It is important to distinguish between the formal expression of the Assembly's commitment to sustainable development in its Sustainable Development Scheme and its practices. One official argued that

"The impact of the Sustainable Development Scheme has been zero. It fulfils the legal duty and that is all."

At a senior level some officials did not want a sustainable development strategy and killed it off. Instead, it is claimed, sustainable development needs to be woven into the fabric, into all the things that the Assembly does. Such views are illustrative of the variability of the degree of buy-in to sustainability both horizontally and vertically within the Assembly (as it does within local government and the ASPBs). As one official from outside the Assembly commented of both his own organisation and the Assembly:

"You cannot ignore environmental issues but for some staff it will be a side issue. But politically you cannot ignore it."

At a political level, there have been a number of instances to show that senior ministers do take an increasingly serious interest in sustainability. For instance, the First Minister's attendance at the World Summit on Sustainable Development in Johannesburg in August 2002 was also warmly welcomed as a mark of the commitment of a senior political figure to sustainable development. One practical outcome of the Summit was the central role played by the Assembly in the Guateng Declaration that established a global network of regional governments committed to sustainable development. According to the Sustainable Development 2003 Annual Report and Action Plan (p9)

> *"We [the Assembly] now find ourselves in a leadership position internationally in sustainable development, which we never expected when making our Scheme. It doesn't mean that we have all the answers. It does mean that we are firmly at the forefront in posing the key questions. We have placed ourselves in a wonderful position to access new best practice world-wide, and thus keep ourselves at the cutting edge of new thinking about sustainable development."*

Whilst such claims may be slightly overblown and not always matched by substance they do indicate the growing public confidence of the Assembly in its engagement with the challenges of sustainability.

Organisationally the Cabinet established a Sub-Committee on sustainable development in May 2001. The First Minister chairs the sub-committee. It is designed to encourage integrated thinking on sustainability at a political level and to drive the Assembly agenda forward. A further indication of the desire of politicians to move towards a more sophisticated level of debate on sustainability was the creation of an Assembly Co-ordinating Group on Sustainable Development. This consists of the Chairs of Assembly Subject Committees and the sustainable development spokespeople from all four parties.

Considerable activity and some highly visible signs of commitment to sustainable development have marked the first term of the Assembly. Within the Assembly there is a belief that sustainability is being mainstreamed (see WAG 2003, p6). However, beneath the surface, as is to be expected, there is variability to be found in the interpretation of sustainability by different parts of the Assembly; the levels of commitment to sustainability; and the activities that different divisions will perform in relation to sustainability. It is thus not surprising that key partners of the Assembly in delivering sustainable development, namely the ASPBs and local government, often get rather mixed, and from their perspective, confusing messages.

Assembly Sponsored Public Bodies: delivering change?

There are a small number of Assembly Sponsored Public Bodies (ASPBs) who have an obvious contribution to make to the Assembly's sustainability strategy. Most notable amongst these are the well-known environmental bodies, the Environment Agency and Countryside Council for Wales. Equally important though will be those ASPBs with an economic remit (like the Welsh Development Agency and Wales Tourist Board) and those with social or cultural responsibilities (such as the National Museums and Galleries of Wales).

For all of the ASPBs devolution has changed their relationship with government, with each other, and to a lesser extent with the NGO community. There is a strong belief amongst the ASPBs that they are less insular than they used to be. The drive towards partnership working means that organisations are more consensual and that there is much more dialogue between them and the Assembly. ASPBs also appear to be more accommodating towards NGOs. This is partly recognition by ASPBs that their credibility on sustainability matters requires legitimisation from the NGO community and partly a genuine desire to engage with partners in progressing sustainability.

Within the Assembly the ASPBs are regarded as part of government and they are 'managed' in a rather different way to that of local government. For local government there is a clear sense that the Assembly must and does regard them as partners but such sensitivities do not apply to the ASPBs. The latter, it is felt within the Assembly, must deliver on the Assembly's programme because "they are part of our stable". The relationship between the Assembly and its ASPBs will involve regular contacts between staff, the issuing of guidance and of course the funding that the Assembly provides for its ASPBs. Important indicators of the messages that the ASPBs receive from the Assembly divisions that are responsible for them are in the corporate plans that the ASPBs produce and in the annual remit letters issued by the Assembly to 'guide' the work of their ASPBs.

Ideally the mainstreaming of sustainable development within the Assembly should lead to consistent messages being provided to its ASPBs. That is not happening and the variability of ASPB experiences may be a reflection of the different contributions that they can make to the pursuit of a more sustainable Wales but is more likely to arise because of two other factors. First, the differing enthusiasms and commitment to sustainability of different parts of the Assembly and the ASPBs for which they are responsible. Second, and potentially highly significant, that sustainability advocates within the Assembly are able to push their message beyond the more receptive environment divisions within the Assembly and their ASPBs to the potentially more challenging economic and social agendas of other departments and ASPBs. For instance, the commitment to sustainable development in the annexes of the remit letters of the Welsh Development Agency and Welsh Tourist Board are potentially a very important indication of the mainstreaming of sustainability within the Assembly.

Underneath the formal engagement between the Assembly and its ASPBs a more complex picture emerges. The ASPBs retain some independence of action and, combined with the myriad of messages that their staff receive from the Assembly, interpret and act on the Assembly's sustainability agenda in at least three different ways. First, for some the Assembly's commitment to sustainable development has been enthusiastically embraced and acted in a very positive manner in progressing their own internal sustainability agenda. A second response from ASPBs is that the Assembly has made little difference to their work either because they were already thinking about sustainability or because they regard themselves as outside of the mainstream of sustainability. Third, some ASPB staff face hostility or indifference to promoting sustainable development within their organisations.

The ASPBs have a key role in delivering the Assembly's sustainable development agenda. From a governance perspective, however, it is clear that there is variability in the extent to which such bodies are currently willing or able to mainstream sustainable development in their activities. Such variability is reinforced, first by the Assembly providing inconsistent messages in its encouragement of ASPBs to deliver on sustainability, and second, by not effectively using the tools to 'manage' its ASPBs to get them to deliver on its agenda.

Local government and sustainability

How has the Assembly fared with local government where a different set of relationships comes into play? As part of the new devolution politics the Government of Wales Act formally strengthened links between the Assembly and local government by placing a duty upon the former to sustain and promote the latter. This commitment has taken a number of forms including a commitment to partnership working and the signing of compacts and policy agreements. Policy agreements, for example, are to be set with individual local authorities to further the aims of Better Wales, a key policy document. The idea behind them is:

> "to facilitate a change in the relationship between local and central government based on agreements focused on the delivery of key policy outcomes as opposed to and led by finance" (WLGA 2000, para 2).

This means that the Assembly will negotiate targets with local authorities, and provide associated funding to meet these targets. However, it is important to note that the WLGA does not wish to see a direct link between funding and individual targets but rather they are seeking:

> "a corporate payment of money as opposed to a target-by-target achievement payment. The presence of hypothecated funding in England means that ring fenced payment by service is acceptable. In Wales the Association feels that this defeats the object of Policy Agreements, which aims for agreements across the board and rewards authority wide corporate performance" (WLGA 2001, para 6).

These negotiations will be underpinned by the Assembly's cross cutting theme of sustainable development. In real terms, this has great potential to influence the local authorities' activities i.e. cash with sustainability strings attached. From a practitioner's point of view, this can provide access to areas of authority activity that would normally be beyond the scope of their remit.

The question that arises then is, do these new arrangements that are meant to ensure more consensual central-local relations based around shared agendas and focused on delivery (i.e. outcomes) rather than simply monitoring inputs (i.e. funding) provide the means to deliver sustainable development at the local level? Whilst the new arrangements may take time to settle down and deliver, the results below do seem to show that there are difficulties in mainstreaming sustainability in local government. This is despite the considerable enthusiasm that exists amongst local government sustainability co-ordinators for the Assembly's sustainable development agenda. Part of the problem appears to be that there is no overall requirement from the Assembly for local government to demonstrate that they are mainstreaming sustainable development.

The results below summarise in tabular form and using selected quotes the views of local government sustainable development officers. The results are presented around four tables:

- Officers' perceptions of Section 121 (Table 2.1)
- The actions that they believe have resulted from Section 121 (Table 2.2)
- Officers' perceptions of the Sustainable Development Compact (Table 2.3)
- The actions that they believe have resulted from the Compact. (Table 2.4)

Table 2.1. Officers' perceptions of the influence of the Sustainable Development Scheme on their authority

Lot of influence	Limited influence	No influence or limited to rhetoric
0	13	8

One of the most enthusiastic comments on the Scheme was:

> *'That we have a Scheme is a major achievement. It has raised the profile of sustainable development and provided opportunities to begin to understand what can be done (e.g. procurement). ... It's like the penny is just dropping. But there is only so much WAG can do. Eighty per cent of delivery of sustainable development is through local authorities and QUANGOs. At the moment it's all talk.'*

Seven of the officers also mentioned, unprompted, that its influence was weakened because the council was receiving confusing messages from the Assembly. A typical comment was:

> *'There is a piecemeal approach from WAG in mainstreaming sustainable development into the agenda. There is evidence from a variety of schemes (Communities First, Health etc) that thinking is not being joined up with WAG and that affects the authority in delivering WAGs aspirations.'*

So, if the Assembly's Scheme is perceived by those in local government who have a responsibility to promote sustainable development as having only a limited impact, where do they believe that it is beginning to make a difference? The results in Table 2.2 below show that there is a process of engagement with sustainability but there are strong implications that it is rather opportunistic rather than systematic. For example, the ideal from the perspective of the sustainability officers would be for them to believe that sustainability is being mainstreamed within their councils but none believed this was happening. Next best would be to influence senior management followed by influencing policies or programmes. Ticking boxes refers to filling in forms, often for Objective 1 bids.

Table 2.2. Officers' perceptions of the actions of their authority as a result of the Sustainable Development Scheme

Mainstream sustainable development	Influence senior management (officers and/or councillors)	Influence policies and/or programmes	Tick boxes
0	3	9	3

So there is progress on the easier areas but much less on the more challenging issues that affect the council as a whole. An officer who could begin to recognise the influence of the Scheme on their council said: 'The SD Scheme has been used to a certain extent to promote this (SD) to senior and middle managers and politicians to drive activity... There is some evidence of the Scheme filtering through the Council's activities'.

Officers were also asked specific questions about the Sustainable Development Compact agreed between the Assembly and the WLGA in July 2002. The aim of the Compact is

"to promote close and harmonious relationships and good communications and to foster constructive co-operation."

It outlines areas where the Assembly and local government will co-operate to deliver policy outputs, and these are education; sustainability appraisal; climate change; community planning and developing quality of life indicators. There are very few commitments within the Compact and rather more aspirational language in the form of 'promoting' and 'encouraging'.

Table 2.3. Officers' perceptions of the influence of the Sustainable Development Compact on their authority

Lot of influence	Limited influence	No influence or limited to rhetoric
0	6	15

Typical comments on the Compact included:

'It is just about protocols. It has no real relevance or direct impact to our work.'

Or

'It's another piece of paper.'

The officers' largely dismissive comments on the influence of the Compact were reflected in their judgements of impact that the Compact had made on their council. The low response from the officers in Table 2.4 below is in large part a reflection of their inability to provide a positive response.

Table 2.4. Officers' perceptions of the actions of their authority as a result of the Sustainable Development Compact

Mainstream sustainable development	Influence policies and/or programmes	Influence senior management (officers and/or councillors)	Tick boxes
0	0	2	3

As one officer commented:

'The weakness is it [the Compact] has no influence on corporate management.'

Local government has been dealing with sustainability issues for well over a decade and has dedicated staff in post to promote local sustainability and who identify with the Assembly's agenda. What emerges, though, is a mismatch between the expectations of staff over what they believe the Assembly should be doing to promote the mainstreaming of sustainability and what they believe is happening within their own organisations. Officers do not believe that there is the external scrutiny of local government and sustainability processes to ensure that senior management is engaged. The Sustainable Development Compact is perceived to have little impact on senior management within their councils. In other words, what we have here is a partnership model of governance that lacks mechanisms for ensuring delivery. The delivery deficit is compounded because the officers also believe that local government is subject to inconsistent messages on sustainable development in different policy areas from the Assembly.

Governance and the delivery of sustainable development

The Assembly is working within a complex network of relationships. It has been faced with a unique policy challenge and this has in turn raised questions about the model of governance it should adopt to deliver its sustainability agenda. Although it is still learning how best to deal with its partners, two extreme options can be drawn from the two ideal types (coercive and partnership) of governance illustrated in Table 2.5 below. The **coercive model** is one that would have been familiar to those used to working under the Assembly's predecessor, the Welsh Office, and which seems to characterise the way in which it thinks of its ASPBs. The **partnership model** is a style of governance to which the Assembly aspires, and one which seems to characterise much of its relationship with local government. In practice, though, these two models will run alongside one another and into one another.

Table 2.5. Delivering sustainable development in Wales: models of governance

Feature	Coercive	Partnership
Targets	Set from centre, prescriptive	Agreed by consent
Means to achieve goals	Hold to account and audit, rule bound relationships	Educate and spread knowledge
Agendas	Likely to be different agendas held by different actors	Seek shared agenda
Lower level autonomy	Minimise local discretion	Accept local discretion and autonomy
Knowledge	Concentrated at the centre and to be dispersed from the centre outwards	Knowledge diffused and seek means to utilise local knowledge
Openness	Limited and to favoured few	Consultative and participatory
Views of lower tier of government/ASPBs	Hierarchy	Partner in policy delivery
Funding	Ring fence budgets	Budgets determined according to local priorities within a common agenda
Policy outcomes	Seek uniformity around a baseline because monitoring for compliance with targets	Accept variability above baseline because seeking improvements in practice and spreading knowledge

The two models of governance clearly involve quite different means for seeking to achieve the goal of sustainability. How might these best be utilised to promote sustainability? What capacities (e.g. power, resources, skills) are required by different participants to utilise these different models? For both the Assembly and its partners the relationships are still new and fluid, and it is perhaps best to say that both sides are engaged in a learning-by-doing exercise.

This brings us to the final point, namely the need to find governance mechanisms to manage and overcome inter-governmental conflicts between the different tiers of the multi-level polity. The potential for such conflict has increased as a result of the twin processes of regionalisation and Europeanisation and this can be illustrated by two emerging controversies in the natural and built environment in Wales.

The first concerns the recently created network of regions which are struggling to remain GMO-free areas, an alliance which includes Upper Austria, Tuscany and Wales and seven others. A GMO-free environment could be said to be part of the Welsh Assembly's duty under section 121 of the Government of Wales Act, but is this duty being undermined by more liberal GM regulations at the EU level? If this is the case, it means that subsidiarity is being drastically curtailed when it is being used to promote sustainability in a country which has a statutory duty to do so.

The second potential conflict concerns the relationship between the Assembly and its local government partners in promoting the Welsh Housing Quality Standard, a major political commitment to upgrade the quality of housing, especially social housing, in Wales. It is becoming increasingly clear that many local authorities, perhaps even the majority, will fail to meet the new quality standard, which for social housing must be met in full by 2012. It is not clear what sanctions, if any, the Assembly has at its disposal to deal with this situation. While partnership is the Assembly's preferred governance model, what will it do when its partners fail to deliver? In England central-local government relationships tend to be biased towards the coercive model, with low trust, adversarial relations and a punitive regulatory regime. Although the Assembly wishes to avoid this model, it will need to prove that 'partnership' is not a soft option for underperforming local authorities. If it does tolerate failure with the Welsh Housing Quality Standard, it will mean that those people with least - council house tenants - will suffer most, and this is a far cry from what the architects of the sustainable development scheme had in mind when they designed this unique duty.

The National Assembly's commitment to sustainable development, especially at the aspirational level, is manifestly clear from the fact that it takes its duty under section 121 very seriously. But the main challenge now for the Assembly and its partners in local government and the public sector is to make the difficult transition from good intentions to good practice, otherwise the social reality will undermine the political rhetoric.

References

Bishop, K and Flynn A (1999) 'The National Assembly for Wales and the Promotion of Sustainable Development: implications for collaborative government and governance', *Public Policy and Administration*, Vol 14, No2, pp62-76.

Chaney, P et al (eds) (2001) *New Governance - New Democracy? Post Devolution Politics in Wales*, University of Wales Press, Cardiff

Corry, D and Stoker, G (2002) *New Localism: Refashioning the Centre-Local Relationship*, New Local Government Network, London

House of Commons (2001) *Making Government Work: The Emerging Issues*, Public Administration Select Committee, HC 94

Flynn, A (2003) *Living Differently? An Assessment of the First Four Years of the Welsh Assembly Government's Sustainable Development Duty*, Cardiff University, The Centre for Business Relationships, Accountability, Sustainability and Society, Working Paper No. 9.

Lamassoure, A (2002) *Draft Report on the Division of Powers Between the EU and the Member States*, Committee on Constitutional Affairs, European Parliament, Brussels

Morgan, K (2002) 'The New Regeneration Narrative: Local Development in the Multi-Level Polity', *Local Economy*, Volume 17 (3), pp. 191-199

Morgan, K and Mungham, G (2000) *Redesigning Democracy: The Making of the Welsh Assembly*, Seren, Bridgend

National Assembly for Wales (2000), *Learning to Live Differently*, November 2000.

Welsh Assembly Government (2003), *Starting to Live Differently*: Consultation on the review of the Sustainable Development Scheme, October 2003.

WLGA (Welsh Local Government Association) (2000) *Co-ordinating Committee*, 15 December, Secretary's report, Enclosure No 5.3.

WLGA (Welsh Local Government Association) (2001) *Co-ordinating Committee*, 29 June, Enclosure No B2.

Chapter 3

Creating Sustainable Food Chains:
The Role of Positive Public Procurement

Kevin Morgan and Adrian Morley

One of the genuinely puzzling things about postwar economic policy in the UK is that successive governments have shown an avid interest in intervening in areas where they have little or no control, like the money markets, while they have virtually ignored areas like public procurement, where they have most control. Perhaps not surprisingly, therefore, the history of public procurement in the UK is littered with costly and embarrassing overruns, notably in defence, IT and civil engineering. Critics might be forgiven for thinking it was forever thus, citing the sorry sagas of the System X digital exchange and the Advanced Passenger Train to underline the point that public procurement has been the Cinderella of economic policy in the UK.

With the creation of the Office of Government Commerce in 2000, the public procurement process is belatedly being modernised to secure value for money improvements across a wide array of government estate. Laudable as it is, however, this modernisation process begs an important question: is public procurement being modernised within an old, cost-cutting business model or does modernisation embrace a new, more sustainable business model? The more it resembles the latter, the more we can speak of a positive public procurement process, a process that is both innovative and sustainable - innovative because it seeks to transform the behaviour of customers and suppliers rather than taking them as given, and sustainable because it does not allow low cost options to masquerade as best value options.

In this chapter we aim to pursue these questions using an unusual case study of public procurement: rather than focusing on the big budget examples of military equipment or information technology, we shall focus on the prosaic case of school meals because it highlights the potential of using positive public procurement to promote the cause of sustainable development. In our view positive public procurement has the potential to secure a multiple dividend in the form of the following benefits:

- More nutritious school food could help to reduce diet-related health problems like obesity, cancer, heart disease and diabetes, diseases which are estimated to cost the NHS some £4 billion annually
- Locally produced school meals could create new local markets for local farmers and producers, affording a lifeline to hard pressed rural areas
- A more localised agri-food chain using organic products could yield environmental benefits, including lower food miles (Morgan and Morley, 2002)

School Meals: A Litmus Test of Sustainable Development

In cultural terms the British school meal has been portrayed in film and literature as something to be endured rather than enjoyed, a character-forming experience for the future elite in public schools and grammar schools alike, and consequently not something to be taken seriously. Indeed, a legacy of smutty jokes about spotted dick and lumpy custard further trivialised the issue, condemning the school meal to comic status. Far from being a trivial matter, however, we argue that the school meal is at the forefront of cutting edge debates about health and well being – so much so that the humble school dinner has become a litmus test of our commitment to sustainable development.

Recent years have given the lie to the stereotype that the British don't care about the quality of their food. Over the past decade there has been a revolution in the quality of British food, with the re-discovery of local and regional products and a new emphasis on fresh ingredients. But there are winners and losers in every revolution and the beneficiaries of this quality revolution tend to be middle class food aficionados and the finer restaurants. The customers of public sector catering – schools, hospitals, care homes and the like – have yet to enjoy the benefits of this quality food revolution, unlike their counterparts in other EU countries (Peckham and Petts, 2003).

But there is now a growing awareness of, and receptivity to the quality of food in what we might call prosaic settings, especially in schools for example. It is not difficult to see why this is happening. In fact the most important reasons can be summed up in two words – health and safety. Perennial food scares have forced consumers to think more carefully about the quality of their food and the conditions under which it is produced. This is a new and encouraging departure because the food chain - that production, processing and logistical nexus that brings our food from farm to fork - is a vast terra incognita to the majority of consumers in Britain.

However, if food chains at the top end of the market are becoming slightly more transparent with regard to provenance of ingredients and methods of production, we remain almost totally ignorant about the food chains which feed the most vulnerable consumers of all – namely pupils and patients.

While schools and hospitals ought to be the epitome of healthy eating environments, getting nutritious food as a matter of course, the reality leaves much to be desired. Such are the cost pressures on public sector caterers that schools and hospitals are forced to operate in low cost food chains, the very chains which have been most prone to food scares. While food-borne diseases arouse the greatest fears among consumers, the truth is that disease-free food, in the shape of unhealthy diets, is a more pervasive threat to health. The burden of food-related ill-health in Britain is both larger than, and different to what it is generally assumed to be. As regards the scale of the problem, food-related ill-health (in the form of cancer, heart disease, stroke, diabetes, obesity and hypertension etc) is estimated to cost the NHS as much as £4 billion a year and, in human terms, it accounts for some 10% of morbidity and mortality. As regards the nature of the problem, however, ill-health due to *unhealthy diets* is reckoned to be some 50 times greater than ill-health due to food-borne diseases (Rayner, 2002).

We cannot dismiss these costs as the inevitable result of 'free choice' on the part of consumers because the latter do not make their choices in a vacuum – and the *social* environment of food choice is overwhelmingly shaped by the fast food industry.

The primary responsibility for re-balancing the social environment of food choice rests squarely with the government because no other body has the mandate or the capacity to undertake such a demanding task – a task that falls within the government's formal commitment to sustainable development, which aims to promote social, economic and environmental well-being. In public policy terms there is something genuinely radical, and perhaps even unique, about sustainable development, which is that it cannot be accomplished through government action alone.

While government is the biggest and most important single player here, effective sustainable development policy needs to be understood as a collective social endeavour. To be effective, in other words, the sustainable development process needs to become a deliberative process of self-management in which people are doing it for themselves, because they value it, rather than having it done for them or to them from above.

But what does this mean in practical terms? In the context of school meals it means that schools (that is parents, teachers, governors, caterers and of course the children themselves) recognise the health and educational benefits of school food and integrate the latter into a whole school approach in which pupils have ample opportunity to learn about food and nutrition in the curriculum in ways that are consistent and self reinforcing (Harvey, 2000).

In the following sections we aim to show that the issue of school meals, far from being a trivial issue, is nothing less than a litmus test of our political commitment to sustainable development. If sustainability is to be a serious organising principle in our societies, a stimulus to us learning to live more sustainable lifestyles, then there is surely no better place to begin than by ensuring that our schools are exemplary healthy eating environments.

A System Under Stress: The School Catering Service Today

Public sector catering is the Cinderella of the catering trade and it therefore tends to be overlooked, even though it is a highly significant part of the food service sector. For example, the public sector in England spends some £1.8 billion per annum on food and catering services. In Wales a total of 92 public sector institutions collectively purchase approximately £60 million on food products each year, but there is little or no co-ordination, hence this procurement power is dissipated. Of this £60 million, local authorities account for over half, followed by the NHS and Higher Education. Within local authority catering provision however, school meals are by far the largest element of their catering duties. It has been estimated that over 180,000 school meals are produced each day for approximately 190 days a year in Wales. This is equivalent to 21.6 million school meals a year. (LACA, 2002).

Our understanding of how school meals services operate and deliver such a fundamentally important service has, however, been limited, despite the growing interest in the broader potential of school meals as a driver for health, well being and sustainable development. This chapter attempts to shed light on these activities by communicating some of the main findings from a study of three local authority run school meal services in Wales: Carmarthenshire, Rhondda Cynon Taff (RCT) and Cardiff. The study highlights the underlying dynamics and drivers of modern public sector procurement and their impact on sustainable development objectives. Also highlighted is the context dependent nature of school meal provision in the UK and how different authorities cope with seemingly conflicting pressures for healthier food provision while retaining interest from their customers (i.e. pupils) and providing better 'value for money' for their paymasters. In particular, we illustrate how the quest for 'value for money' imposed by regimes such as Compulsory Competitive Tendering (CCT) and Best Value have stripped sustainability out of school meals.

The study took place within the context of increasing choice for individual schools as to how their meal services are run. Fair Funding legislation came into force in April 2000, allowing individual schools to assume control of their own school meals budgets. In effect, this provided schools with three alternatives as to how to meet their responsibilities for school meal provision:

- The development of service level agreements with their existing in-house council school meal provider (either on an individual basis or groups of schools under one agreement)
- Sub-contract the provision of school meals to a private contractor (again either on an individual basis or groups of schools)
- Run their meal provision themselves, including procurement activities

In practice, across Wales the vast majority of schools has so far retained their traditional in house service providers. In fact, virtually the entire primary school sector in Wales has kept council providers. Some secondary schools, both individually and on a Local Authority basis, however, have brought in commercial businesses. Torfaen, for example, subcontracted all its secondary schools service in this way. Such contracts tend to be won by large, often multinational firms such as Sodexho or Scolarest. The third option is virtually unknown in Wales at the moment, although examples exist across England.

In-house catering providers can be generalised as having centralised procurement structures and control over aspects such as pricing structures and nutritional targets. Catering managers within schools however, often have the power to vary menus somewhat to suit their individual needs. In general, in-house catering providers have service level agreements with each school. Table 3.1 presents a series of key facts about the three authority run services investigated. The figure illustrates the scale of operations involved with each of the services.

Table 3.1. A Profile of the School Catering Case Studies

	Carmarthenshire County Catering Service	Catering Direct (Rhondda Cynon Taff)	Cardiff Catering
Primary & Special School Meals	139 Primary, 2 Special	144 Primary, 4 Special	114 Primary, 7 Special
Comprehensive School Meals	14 Comprehensive	19 Comprehensive	20 Comprehensive
Volume	Approximately 22,000 meals a day	Approximately 33,000 meals a day	Approximately 25,000 meals a day
Catering Turnover	£7 Million	Approximately £8 Million	£7 Million
Food Expenditure	£3 Million	£7 Million*	£2.5 Million
No. of Staff	720	945	800
Percentage Uptake	67% Primary 80% Comprehensive	49% Primary 62% Comprehensive	50% Primary 46% Comprehensive

* Figure includes three other neighbouring authorities.

The three services were chosen to reflect the diversity of contexts within which school meals providers operate. Cardiff Catering function in a multicultural urban context with a broad socio-economic customer base. Carmarthenshire, by contrast, is a largely rural area with a relatively strong interest in farming issues. The county also has exceptionally high school meal take-up rates. RCT is part of the South Wales industrial heartland, which contains areas of high unemployment and relative public health problems.

Cost Primacy and The Degradation of Sustainable School Meal Provision

Subjecting public services to competitive pressures has forced them to act more and more like private enterprises. Community food provision, whether through schools, hospitals or community care has not escaped this process. In fact, catering along with leisure services are the most commercially run parts of modern councils. Local authority caterers are forced to operate as if they were private businesses, even though their wider objectives - to meet basic standards of nutrition and to promote healthy eating for example - sit uncomfortably with these narrow commercial pressures. If they are unable to compete then they risk losing their operations to private sector companies.

In Carmarthenshire, for example, cafeterias in comprehensive schools are run as businesses. They do not even get a traditional budget from the council but rather a trading account, which has to be balanced each year by income generation. Income for school meal providers originates from money paid directly by pupils and free school meal grants. From these revenues they have to cover all costs. In Carmarthenshire, the service also has to work towards a target surplus (i.e. profit) each year. In 2002/03, the target figure was £139,000. Although this amount is re-invested into school meal provision, both at the council level and by individual schools, it remains a driver towards ever decreasing costs in the service. In fact, school meals providers are committed to improving their service continually year on year in all areas, but particularly in cost terms. One large comprehensive school in Carmarthenshire recently received a cheque for £12,000, as a share of the profit generated in its canteen.

Consequently, cost has become the key operational factor for school meals providers. The scale of operations dictates that even small increases in ingredient costs can have a major impact on the financial performance of the provider. For example, Cardiff Catering were recently over-spending by 3p on each meal due to supplier problems. This translated to a loss of approximately £16,000 each month.

The Growth of Processed Foods

The predominance of cost as a contract criterion impacts on small businesses in two key ways. Firstly, it is apparent that in most cases large firms are simply able to produce food more cheaply than their small counterparts. Despite having to incur greater transportation costs, economies of scale and production efficiencies enable large firms to compete more effectively on a cost basis. Secondly, and in many ways more importantly, cost pressures impact on the types of food purchased. Public sector caterers have increasingly had to purchase processed or pre-prepared food ingredients as they are more cost effective. This is largely a consequence of the gradual change in balance between food costs and labour costs. While the relative (immediate) cost of food has decreased, the cost of labour in the UK has increased. This means that overall cost reduction is more achievable by reducing labour costs in food production processes rather than material costs. Therefore, it has made economic sense within the food industry as a whole to take out labour involvement through increasing aggregated food processing using capital intensive techniques. This has been one of the key drivers for the growth in the food processing industry over recent decades.

Within the school meals service also, procurers have increasingly purchased processed food at the expense of catering staff hours. An example of this is potato chips. All three councils studied buy in semi-cooked chilled chips (called 'frites' in the catering trade). In the past school catering staff would have prepared chips themselves from whole potatoes. In the modern day, this is not a viable proposition. Buying in whole potatoes and preparing them on site requires kitchen staff to scrub them, put them through peeling machines, hand cut them and then put them into a chipper.

There are also other factors that influence the trend towards purchasing processed foods in schools. Cardiff, for example, illustrated the problem of labour shortages, particularly for skilled cooks, that can influence school meals providers to rely on labour as little as possible. In addition, many small schools have lost their kitchens. Centralised production is inherently more attuned to efficiencies associated with processed food. Perishability is also an important influence. It is generally harder to handle and to ensure the quality of fresh food compared with processed alternatives, particularly in large industrial kitchens.

A final factor that influences the trend towards processed food procurement has been simply children's tastes. School meal providers have had to reflect broader consumption habits among children towards products such as burgers, chicken nuggets and confectionery that are much easier to buy in rather than to prepare on-site. This trend is regarded by many in the school meals service as being partially a result of television adverts for these kinds of products during children's television programming.

The increasing use of processed food in school meals impacts directly on both the health of children and the prospects of increased relocalisation. In terms of health, it is far more difficult for school meal providers to control levels of fat, sugar, protein, vitamins etc when they purchase cheap processed food. Fat and sugar in particular are often used by the food industry essentially as cost saving ingredients as they enhance flavour and texture cheaply. Similarly, artificial flavours, colours and preservatives are often cost saving alternatives to natural ingredients or, in the case of preservatives, necessary to prolong the shelf life of the product in order for it to get from the factory to the child's plate. In addition there are issues associated with saturated fat, excessive water levels in meat products and nutritional loss during processing and storage.

The use of processed foods also reduces the scope for small local producers to win public sector contracts. Processed foods require supply chain infrastructure, particularly processing equipment. Much industrial sized food processing is done by computer controlled machinery that requires high capital investment and the availability of technical expertise. Consequently, much processing, particularly for low value high throughput foods, is done by large processing plants often located in geographical clusters around the UK. Processed foods are also more likely to be branded, even for products used in public catering. Successful branding requires relatively high investment both in money and expertise. By purchasing more processed foods, public institutions are also diminishing locality as a quality factor as processing invariably includes shelf life extension. It follows therefore, that small firms are less able to compete with large remote businesses in processed foods than they are for fresh products.

Carmarthenshire attributes the success of its school meals service, in terms of the high take up rates, to the use of fresh ingredients and in-school preparation of food. Over the years the service has managed to retain both the equipment needed and the appropriate cooking skills among its staff. According to the head of the school meals service, the retention of these two assets, along with strong commitment among staff, has enabled them to readdress the balance between labour and food costs. Consequently, labour costs are higher than in other authorities but they are more able to produce meals from scratch. This in turn has brought very high levels of take up rates across the county and enabled the service providers better to control the healthiness of the meals served.

The case of Carmarthenshire however, seems to be the exception rather than the rule. Although CCT triggered this trend towards cheaper processed food and the related loss of kitchens and cooking skills among staff, Best Value, regarded by many as a more flexible, less cost-focused regime also drives in-house school meal providers in much the same direction. As Table 3.2 illustrates, the Best Value review of Carmarthenshire's Catering Service concluded with a number of recommendations that had the effect of moving the school meals service away from fresh, home-made food. Moreover, under the terms of Best Value, the council is obliged to pursue the report's recommendations.

Table 3.2. Carmarthenshire Best Value Inspectors Report for Catering Services (2001)

The Best Value review undertaken by Carmarthenshire County Council Catering Service in 2001 provides a rich example of the evolutionary reform pressures faced by council run school meals services in the UK. It is also particularly illuminating in light of the particular effort the service has made over the years to retain the production of as much home-made food, using fresh ingredients, as possible. Under Best Value, the service had to benchmark itself against similar services in other councils. If a service does not compete then the provider must set out a development plan which outlines how it will improve performance.

The inspectors report of CCC's Best Value review awarded the service 2 stars for the standard of service (from a range of 0 – 3 stars) and concluded it was likely to improve further as a result of the review process. The inspectors characterised the service as one of 'High Quality High Cost' and praised the service for the range and quality of food available and the standard of front line staff. The review however, emphasised that productivity levels were particularly low in primary school kitchens and should therefore be tackled. Although not stated explicitly in the official report, poor productivity can be assigned to the high degree of preparation and cooking in the kitchens of Carmarthenshire's schools compared to other authorities. Among the key recommendations of the Best Value review was that productivity be improved.

In effect the review was recommending that less food preparation be done in school kitchens, or in other words, the council should purchase more processed food. This highlights the impact that auditing priorities and associated procedures can have on the ability of school meals providers to purchase local fresh food. One of the operational conclusions was that efforts should be made to further drive down food costs. The report states that 'if productivity cannot be improved

Figure 3.2. Carmarthenshire Best Value Inspectors Report for Catering Services (2001) Continued

and if competitiveness cannot be demonstrated then the council is committed to engaging the private sector or other partners in the delivery of the service'. As a result of the review the service committed itself to a productivity study in primary school kitchens and to consider purchasing pre-prepared vegetables to reduce production times. They stated that, as a result of the review 'it will be necessary to investigate the option of buying in pre-prepared vegetables from an external fruit and vegetable suppliers, as opposed to the time consuming current method'. In terms of the balance between labour and food costs, the Best Value review concluded that the service had to try to cut staff costs as they were higher than any other authority. This was largely because they had kept to 'national conditions of service' within the council. Hence both pay and conditions are in excess of the private sector. However, because other councils with which Carmarthenshire was being benchmarked, had driven below these conditions, CCC was urged to follow suit. Here we have a perfect illustration of a school catering service trying to put sustainable development principles into practice - only to find itself being pushed in the opposite direction by Best Value.

Source: Audit Commission; 2001 CCC

Fewer Suppliers Equals Lower Transaction Costs

Many of the problems associated with procuring from local businesses – put forward by public procurement professionals – do not pertain to individual businesses so much as to envisaged situations of having to deal with large numbers of small local businesses. Dealing with such situations would present a series of challenges to modern day procurement priorities. Perhaps the most critical is the administrative burden caused by processing a large number of invoices. In Carmarthenshire, just nine suppliers generate over 2000 invoices every week. Anything like a return to the pre-CCT situation when they had 64 suppliers would generate significantly more invoices.

Every invoice that accompanies a delivery to a school has to be checked and then posted to the council, where it is batched, processed and input. It is then transferred to county hall for authorisation and payment from the ledger, which has to be updated. In fact, reducing transaction costs has been a strong driver for saving money across councils in recent years.

Working with a larger number of small producers also presents problems associated with modern demands for comprehensive quality systems. Not only are small businesses likely to differ in how they administer their quality systems, councils have also experienced wide variations in standards among businesses. Modern councils require comprehensive audit trails for their food products. RCT for example, tries to audit all its suppliers at least once a year on issues such as quality assurance, training, hygiene, health and safety.

Moreover, Quality Assurance is even more important for council catering providers because they have vulnerable client bases (children and often old people). In RCT, if they have problems with suppliers they will often offer their own services to train staff. This approach is feasible with a handful of suppliers, but may not be so with a much broader supply base. A larger number of small suppliers may also have a detrimental effect in terms of the number of deliveries to schools. The number of lorries and vans on school premises is an issue that concerns many schools.

Small Businesses Are Not (Currently) Equipped to Play the Game

Among the procurement professionals consulted for the study there was a unanimous conviction that many small businesses lose out because they simply do not understand the specific needs of public institutions. This lack of understanding runs the other way too, since procurement managers do not appreciate the extent to which public procurement procedures have become systematically biased towards large corporate suppliers and against their smaller counterparts.

There appears to be a clear need for training to be provided to help small businesses understand the needs of public institutions, particularly with respect to tendering processes. Contracts tend to be renewed once every 3 to 5 years. This provides only a small window of opportunity for small businesses to gear themselves towards making a bid. It is often the perception that small firms fail to prepare adequately for tendering processes. For example, it was noted in Carmarthenshire that they rarely enquire beforehand when future tenders are due to be invited, and those that are received often appear to be rushed out. Small firms clearly have a disadvantage in terms of tendering expertise and experience compared to large businesses. Firms with a national presence periodically bid for public contracts and therefore can build up experience in tendering processes and often employ people specifically for these activities. A small business, by contrast, may only have the opportunity once every five years to bid for a school meals contract.

Similarly, large firms have dedicated marketing departments and are able to offer broader marketing support to large institutions. In small firms, it is often the owner / manager who takes on the role of marketing. It is not feasible for small firms to employ marketing professionals and invest in support materials when they have no guarantee of winning a large public contract.

Localised production of raw ingredients, such as meat and vegetables, also brings issues of seasonality and price fluctuation. Modern public procurement requires that suppliers can guarantee consistent supply year round. Moreover, because services are running to extremely tight budgets, price fluctuations have to be minimal. One of the authorities described their difficulties with purchasing Welsh lamb because of price fluctuations on the market. Most of the time New Zealand lamb is simply cheaper and more consistent in price terms. In fact, Welsh lamb tends to only be used on an ad hoc basis, when prices are low and then only 'anonymously' as mince in dishes such as moussaka.

Relocalising Opportunities for Small Local Businesses

As the previous section illustrates, in modern public procurement the odds are stacked clearly against fresh food and small local producers. The most effective solution to this problem would undoubtedly be the investment of greater resources into the system that could allow school meals services to reinvest in kitchen equipment that has been lost over previous decades. Resources could be allocated to attract skilled kitchen staff back into the service from the private sector where they currently receive better pay and conditions. Existing staff could also be skilled up to meet the needs. Extra money in the service would also allow procurers to purchase higher quality ingredients of a greater nutritional standard and without many of the cheapening agents that blight much of the food industry.

Clearly these kind of developments could not be sustained without a radically different benchmarking process, not merely in terms of Best Value reviews, but also with respect to the internal performance indicators employed by local authorities. These need to accommodate better the delicate balance between cost, efficiency and quality. Food, nutrition and the provision of health education are too complex to be adequately appraised by universal benchmarking procedures, especially if the latter are based on desiccated value for money considerations.

Getting Ahead Together: Opportunities for Cooperatives

There are also a number of clear steps that can be taken within existing procurement practices in the public sector. Representatives from RCT, in particular, advocate the potential for producer cooperatives to supply public institutions. Cooperatives, and other forms of producer groups, hold two distinct advantages: firstly, they have the potential to bid for whole contracts, avoiding 'cherry picking' scenarios. Secondly, because they are able to invoice centrally, they significantly reduce transaction costs, vis a vis working with large numbers of independent small businesses.

As outlined above, modern council catering services aim to reduce transaction costs wherever possible. They are unlikely to accept dealing with 15 or 20 invoices when they could have only one. Local producer cooperatives however, would seem to be better suited for some product groups than others. RCT, for example, see potential in their area for cooperatives in beef and milk. In fact, in the past, RCT has attempted to persuade local dairies to come together and submit a common tender for their milk contract, without success.

Producers considering coming together to form cooperatives, however, face a dilemma. Establishing a producer cooperative can be a costly exercise, in time, money and independence. Therefore without a strong belief that they will actually win any of the public contracts that they set themselves up for, it may be difficult to persuade them to come together in the first place. Clear encouragement both centrally and from the public institution involved is therefore needed.

An alternative strategy is to encourage local sourcing via existing nominated suppliers. This solution minimises transaction costs (invoices) accrued to the public institution and allows producers to do what they are best at, producing. This is a strategy that has been effectively employed in South Gloucestershire as a means of increasing the amount of local food in schools. These kind of actions already exist among the case study authorities. In RCT, for example, if procurement officers come across a product they feel is suitable they will often request their nominated distributor to develop a relationship with them. This kind of approach, while holding potential, does have a number of drawbacks. It requires a proactive approach from procurement officers and an accommodating stance from existing distributors. Bringing in producers in this manner also causes immediate displacement of existing products. This may present problems for relationships between distributors and their suppliers. This is compounded by the fact that many distributors are also producers of the product. In addition to the time and effort required, for what may be perceived as little immediate benefit to both procurers and distributors, this kind of approach is also limited in scope. If the distributor is a national operator (such as 3663 for example) it is unlikely to be able to accommodate local producers in its existing structures. These problems are similar to those of small businesses trying to deal with supermarkets.

It is clear that, on the whole, the school meal system in the UK has developed in a way that works against the development of sustainable food supply chains. As the preceding sections illustrate, the reasons for this are complex. The underlying factor however has been the gradual squeezing of cost out of the school meal system at the expense of quality, traceability and opportunity for local communities. This process has manifested itself in a number of ways:

- A reduction in the use of fresh produce.
- An increase in use of frozen, pre-prepared and processed foods.
- A loss of kitchen infrastructure in schools.
- A reduction in the numbers and skill levels of catering staff.
- Purchasing on the basis of lowest price with little emphasis on provenance.
- The use of larger contracts and consortia to increase market power and reduce transaction costs.
- An increased emphasis on value adding requirements from suppliers.

Each of these factors acts against the sustainability of communities by impacting not only on the health of school children but also on the opportunities for local businesses and the local workforce. This illustrates the consequences of giving initial cost such primacy, and more specifically, of underplaying the importance of a broad sustainable development approach to public service delivery. However, while local authorities should be encouraged to pursue creative or positive procurement in the name of community well being, there is only so much they can do through their own efforts. As we show in the following section, *positive procurement* is only one ingredient in the recipe for healthy eating and sustainable food chains, and it cannot be effective unless it is combined with other complementary ingredients.

From Good Intentions to Good Practice: Delivering the New Agenda

The school meal service helps us to understand two of the crucial connections that lie at the heart of sustainable development thinking. The first is the physical connection between diet, health and well being, a connection that is all too often acknowledged in theory only to be breached in practice so far as schools are concerned. However, the burgeoning financial costs of treating diet-related diseases, coupled with the escalating moral panic about childhood obesity, will hopefully persuade politicians that the status quo is not a viable option for the future and that healthy eating environments and sustainable food chains are less costly (in human *and* financial terms) than a narrow economic reckoning might suggest. Indeed, if we think in terms of a broader, more sustainable economic metric it can be argued that the school meal service is as much an investment as a cost on account of its contribution to the nation's health (Morgan, 2003).

But the school meal service also illustrates another, equally important connection and that is the political connection between design and delivery. In other words the grand vision of sustainable development is worthless if it is not woven into the prosaic practices of everyday life, especially in schools, where the 'healthy eating' agenda needs to inform the canteen no less than the classroom. According to Marion Nestle, a leading US-based nutritionist, only three things are needed for a healthy school meals service:

- a committed food service director
- a supportive principal
- interested parents (Nestle, 2002)

No doubt a lot can be achieved through a triple alliance of this kind; in actual fact this is the 'secret' behind the islands of good practice in the UK at the moment. But a healthy school meals service which is *sustainable* (i.e. one which uses local and organic food) and systemic (i.e. one which exists throughout the country) will require more concerted action if healthy eating and sustainable food chains are ever to become mainstream activities in the UK. Indeed, nothing short of the concerted actions summarised in the *Healthy Eating Action Plan* in Table 3.3 will create a genuinely healthy eating environment. To appreciate the scale of the challenge of creating a healthy eating environment let us elaborate on each of the components of the action plan in Table 3.3, an action plan which requires complementary actions at a number of different spatial scales, from the global to the local.

Table 3.3. A Healthy Eating Action Plan

Improve the Regulatory Framework
- Taking advantage of CAP reform, and the Treaty commitment to sustainable development, create a regulatory framework in the EU which fosters rather than frustrates the growth of local food economies.
- Create a clearer, more supportive regulatory framework in the UK to encourage re-localisation at all stages of the food chain, especially with respect to public procurement regulations.
- Ensure that local food systems are protected globally by making WTO rules more compatible with nutrition, environmental protection and animal welfare.
- Ensure hygiene and health & safety regulations are appropriate to business size and supportive of local consumption.

Stimulate demand for local food
- Promote consumer education on the benefits of local food and the need to "eat less, move more".
- Raise awareness of the diet-related problems of food of low nutritional value (LNV).
- Public procurement, especially in schools and hospitals, should use local or organic food whenever possible.
- Persuade supermarkets to do more to stock local food and make it more readily available.

Develop the supply of local food
- Develop a supply chain infrastructure to support the local food sector by creating a network of small abattoirs, processing facilities and dairies in each region.
- Use public procurement to encourage small producers to "act big" by working in concert.

Facilitate healthy food choices
- Tax foods and drinks of LNV.
- Require fast food firms to provide better nutritional information on their products.
- Restrict TV adverts for foods and drinks of LNV.
- Ban/reduce the sale of foods and drinks of LNV in schools and facilitate access to water.
- Use health-promoting schools networks to disseminate good practice.

Towards a Healthy Eating Action Plan

Creating a **regulatory framework** that fosters rather than frustrates the growth of sustainable food chains is perhaps the most important reform of all because it creates a new set of incentives and sanctions for everyone in the food chain. The regulatory changes identified in Table 3.3 involve a combination of global action (like the reform of WTO rules to make them more supportive of human health, the environment and animal welfare) and EU action (like further and more radical reform of the Common Agricultural Policy reform to shift the emphasis to sustainable agriculture). But the biggest regulatory barrier to more sustainable food chains, and that means more *localised* food chains, lies in the EU's formidably arcane public procurement directives, which are thought to prohibit public bodies from specifying local food in catering contracts above a certain threshold value. Public procurement managers in the UK have convinced themselves that they cannot procure local food from local producers because their hands are tied by EU directives that forbid such practices on the grounds that they violate the free trade principles of transparency and non-discrimination.

In an earlier publication we addressed the room for manoeuvre within these public procurement directives at great length (Morgan and Morley, 2002). Among other things we were able to show that while the EU directives do indeed outlaw explicit 'buy local' policies from public bodies in member states, some of the latter were being more creative than the UK in how they interpreted the EU directives. For example, public bodies in Italy and France will design contracts that specify certain product qualities – like fresh ingredients, seasonal produce, locally certified products (like those with Protected Geographical Indication status), organic products and so forth – which allow their cities and regions to practise 'buy local' policies in all but name. As a result of such policies many Italian cities now have well-established organic school meal systems in place: in Ferrara, for example, 80% of all food served to the city's nursery schools is organic, while Udine was one of the first Italian cities to supply organic meals to all its schools.

The UK public procurement profession claims that cost is the other big barrier to the use of higher quality food in school meals, and there is much more substance to this charge. Although the average price of a school meal in 2002 was £1.56, most parents would be shocked to discover that just 35 pence is the average amount allocated per child to the actual food for a two-course primary school meal in the UK today. Although 35 pence is nowhere near enough to provide a truly nutritious school meal, most members of the Local Authorities Caterers Association (LACA) seem to perform a minor miracle daily by making these meagre resources go a long way.

A 'cheap food' culture was systematically introduced into the school meal service in the 1980s, when local authorities were exposed to CCT, a market-driven regulatory regime that spawned a cost-cutting mindset which had adverse effects on children and caterers. So far as children were concerned CCT had negative effects on diet, health, choice and portions, while caterers suffered from reduced staff numbers, fewer in-house kitchen facilities and plummeting pay and morale (Unison, 2002). Although New Labour jettisoned some of the cruder, more debilitating features of the CCT regime when it introduced the more enabling *Best Value* regulatory regime, the 'cheap food' culture of CCT lingers on in the school meal service.

Clearly, the regulatory barriers to healthy eating and sustainable food chains are not confined to (real or imagined) EU regulations. Procurement managers in the UK feel that local government regulations are no less ambiguous as to whether they allow local authorities to re-localise their food procurement on sustainability grounds. Apart from *Best Value* constraints, there are the additional constraints of Section 17 of the *Local Government* Act 1988, which sets out a number of 'non-commercial matters' which must be excluded from the contract process. But regulations are never set in aspic. Just as EU procurement regulations are evolving in response to an internal tussle between the twin goals of competition and sustainability, so too are UK local government regulations. In the latter case the tussle is between the competitive concerns of Section 17 of the *Local Government Act 1988* and Part 1 of the *Local Government Act 2000*, which empowers local authorities to promote the social, economic and environmental well-being of their communities.

The key point to make about the above regulatory ambiguities is that, in the UK at least, they foster a risk averse culture: if procurement managers think they are entering a grey zone between legality and illegality when they try something novel and innovative, like promoting sustainable food chains, they will recoil from experimentation, preferring the comfort zone of custom and practice (Morgan and Morley, 2002). For all these reasons, a regulatory framework that offers clearer signals, that supports rather than stymies innovation, is an essential component of any action plan to promote healthy eating and sustainable food chains.

A better informed and more resolute public sector procurement profession could help to boost **demand** for local food, the second component of the action plan in Table 3.3. Far from being the Cinderella of the catering sector that it is in the UK, the public sector catering service in other EU countries has played a significant role in promoting healthy eating and sustainable food chains. Schools, colleges, hospitals, care homes, central and local government, the armed forces collectively constitute an enormous market and this could be used to induce the growth of more localised food chains throughout the UK. A very positive step in this direction was made in August

2003 when DEFRA launched a sustainable food procurement initiative – but initiatives are the beginning not the end of the process.

Stimulating demand for local food is a long-term endeavour and, to be effective, it needs to be part of a wider process of consumer education. But this process of consumer education needs to move beyond the conventional injunctions of the health promotion industry to 'eat less, move more' and to 'beware of foods high in salt, fat and sugar', even though these remain the key messages. Here the UK has much to learn from Italy, where local food products are being used as learning materials for teachers and pupils alike in a programme called 'culture that feeds'. Aside from learning about local produce, and how it changes through the seasons, the key aim of this educational programme is to create knowledgeable consumers, that is consumers who have an awareness of, as well as a commitment to locally-produced nutritious food. Discerning and demanding consumers are ultimately the most important factor of all in the campaign to create *and* maintain healthy eating environments.

However, if more locally-produced nutritious food was demanded in school meals tomorrow it could not be delivered. Why? Simply because farmers and producers are not tooled up to produce it. Nor are the distribution networks available to deliver it. This underlines the significance of the third component of Table 3.3, which is the urgent need to develop a *supply-side capacity* to produce local and nutritious foods. The dangers of creating a new market, by stimulating demand, and doing nothing to create a local source of supply would provoke a flood of imports, making it that much harder for domestic firms to enter the new market. This is precisely what happened with the rapid growth of the UK organic food market, where some 75% of organic products are now supplied through imports.

Local farmers and producers have found it difficult if not impossible to break into the public sector catering market, where the barriers to entry include an exacting tendering process, which is too daunting for small traders, and the caterers' preference for dealing with large national food suppliers, which offer lower transaction costs and sponsorship deals which offer the 'brands' to help hard-pressed school caterers fight-off the challenge of high street competitors. Such is the growth of commercial sponsorship in schools that an influential report on school meals policy in Scotland has recommended that education services should be encouraged to 'de-brand their service' (Scottish Executive's Expert Panel 2002).

This brings us to the final component of Table 3.3, namely the urgent need to promote a *healthy food choice environment*, which includes some of the most controversial proposals in the action plan because they directly impinge on the interests of the junk food industry. Reforming the social environment of food choice, to ensure that healthy food is no longer the pygmy to the fast food giant, is a vital macro-level action to complement the micro-level actions in the food chain. The simple point to make about this complex area of food choice is that we do not make our choices in a vacuum. On the contrary, just 0.9% of the UK food advertising budget in 2000 was devoted to fresh fruit and vegetables; 28% was devoted to advertising cereals, cakes, biscuits, crisps and snacks; and, even more extraordinary, 99% of adverts for food during children's TV programmes were for products high in either salt, sugar or fat (Sustain, 2001).

Although there are some encouraging signs of progress here – like the European Commission's plans for tighter food labelling regulations so as to promote better nutritional information and prohibit spurious health claims – successive UK governments have fought shy of introducing tougher regulations on the junk food industry. As the scale of the childhood obesity epidemic becomes clearer, however, the escalating costs and the moral panic might combine to force government to introduce new curbs on foods and drinks of low nutritional value. Without the concerted actions proposed in Table 3.3 the UK will never be able to emulate the healthy eating environments of other EU member states. Some schools will of course forge ahead with or without a national action plan, but these will remain islands of good practice, the exceptions that prove the rule. These islands of good practice owe their success to the remarkable actions of a few highly committed public sector entrepreneurs. Some local education authorities have also won recognition for their efforts to generalise the provision of high quality school meals through the use of local food, and here we could mention two rural LEAs, Carmarthenshire County Council in West Wales and South Gloucestershire in the South West of England, as exemplars of good practice. But the real challenge is how to extend these success stories to the country at large.

Although the locally-sourced school meal would seem to be a simple confection, it is proving to be a real challenge for everyone involved in the food chain – regulators, producers, suppliers, caterers, procurement managers and parents among many others. Perhaps this is because it challenges some powerful conventions, like the notion that food has to be globally traded, that the provenance of food is unimportant or that cost takes precedence over quality in public sector catering. But in promoting the school as a healthy eating environment, where locally produced nutritious food is *routinely* available, and where pupils, parents and caterers appreciate its benefits, local authorities will be rising to the larger challenge of promoting community well being by weaving sustainable development principles into the warp and weft of everyday life. In other words there's more to the locally sourced school meal than meets the eye.

References

Audit Commission (2001) *Carmarthenshire County Council – Catering Service*, Best Value Inspection Service Wales, Cardiff

Harvey, J (2000) *The Chips Are Down: A Guide to Food Policy in Schools*, Health Education Trust, Stockport

LACA (2002) *Draft Nutritional Strategy for Wales*, Local Authority Caterers Association, Cardiff

Morgan, K (2003) *Time To Recognise School Meals Are An Investment Not Just a Cost*, The Western Mail, 11 June

Morgan, K and Morley, A (2002) *Re-localising the Food Chain: The Role of Creative Public Procurement*, The Regeneration Institute, Cardiff University

Nestle, M (2002) *Food Politics: How the Food Industry Influences Nutrition and Health*, University of California Press, Berkeley

Peckham, C and Petts, J (2003) Good Food on the Public Plate: *A Manual for Sustainability in Public Sector Food and Catering*, Sustain, London

Rayner, M (2002) *The Burden of Food-Related Ill-Health in the UK*, Agri-Food Network Paper, Sustain, London

Scottish Executive's Expert Panel on School Meals (2002) *Hungry for Success: A Whole School Approach to School Meals in Scotland*, Edinburgh

Sustain (2001) *TV Dinners: What's Being Served Up By the Advertisers?*, Sustain, London

Unison (2002) *The School Meals Service in the 21st Century*, Unison Education Services, London

Chapter 4

Sustainable Construction in Practice: The Case of Wales

Caroline Cohen and John Ryder

Introduction

Given the Welsh Assembly Government's (WAG) constitutional commitment to promote Sustainable Development (SD), the current development of the construction sector in economic, social and environmental terms in Wales is an interesting issue, considering its importance for the Welsh economy and its significant impact on the environment.

The Place of the Construction Sector in the Assembly's Sustainable Development Agenda

According to the Welsh Assembly Government's National Economic Development Strategy *'A Winning Wales'*, the construction industry contributed some 5.2% to the Welsh GDP in 1998 and employed some 61,000 people in Wales in 2000. The industry is in a period of transition with the advent of a new EU and UK-wide *Sustainable Construction Agenda* and especially with the emerging European Directive on Energy Performance in Buildings, which brings about changes in the organisation and structure of the sector (DEFRA, 2003).

Under Section 121 of the Government of Wales Act 1998, there is bestowed on the Assembly a responsibility for sustainable development that is unique for an elected body in Britain. The section states that

> *"The Assembly shall make a scheme setting out how it proposes, in the exercise of its functions, to promote sustainable development."*

If the political and policy changes in Wales are matters of substance then they should be reflected in the development of construction policies. Therefore, on two counts, differences should emerge between Wales and other parts of the UK. On one hand, devolution should ensure that Welsh policy makers are sensitive to the circumstances surrounding the construction sector in Wales. On the other hand, the Assembly's commitment to promoting sustainable development should mean that its construction policies are imbued with a philosophy of sustainability. A key research question is, therefore, to what extent can differences in construction policy and management between Wales and other parts of the UK be observed?

Despite the importance of the sector in the region, the Assembly has not developed a strategy specifically aimed at the construction sector in the way it has done to address sustainable waste management issues. There is a lack of strategic guidance - on how best to promote business opportunities in the construction sector, how to foster a supply chain approach amongst local authorities and businesses and how to regenerate the sector which is undergoing a period of transition - in trying to adapt to the new sustainable construction agenda. The Welsh Assembly Government has not helped the sector to adapt effectively to recent and forthcoming legal requirements (mostly addressing environmental issues such as energy and resource efficiency). Rather, there are a plethora of un-coordinated schemes in Wales undertaken by business support organisations of various kinds that are Assembly Sponsored Public Bodies (ASPBs).

It is questionable whether the absence of policy leadership from the Assembly Government on Sustainable Construction (SC) issues reflects a certain crisis of the construction sector in Wales. It is worth looking at the way in which the devolved administration addresses the EU and UK-wide Sustainable Construction agenda, which remains ill-defined and often poorly understood by stakeholders from the public and private sectors. One key issue that arises is whether the Welsh Assembly Government has the means or willingness to implement a comprehensive and indigenous policy framework for SC which reflects the region's attributes and needs. A key concern is the industry's awareness (or lack of it) in applying the principles of Sustainable Development to construction-related activities. Two questions can be considered. First, to what extent is the Assembly capable of implementing a strategy to address the key challenges of the sector? Second, in what way does it attempt to bring various stakeholders together and establish a robust construction network? The underpinning theme of this chapter is to look at the approach taken by the WAG towards the construction sector and to evaluate whether the organisational structures that exist in Wales enable strategic and operational goals and targets to be achieved.

Implications of Sustainable Development for the Construction Sector

The UK government has recognised the impact of the construction sector on the environment and the critical role it has to play to further sustainable forms of economic development. Some of the main environmental issues include energy, resource consumption and waste generation. Energy produced from non-renewable sources and consumed in building services accounts for approximately 50% of UK CO_2 emissions, contributing to climate change, consuming non-renewable resources and adding to pollution. Waste from construction and demolition materials and soil amounts to 70 million tonnes annually; 13 million tonnes of this consists of material delivered to sites but never used. In addition, 90% of non-energy minerals extracted in UK are supplied as materials. It is also worth noting that the industry produces annually 3 times the waste produced by all UK households combined (DTI, 2003a).

In April 2000, the UK Department of the Environment, Transport and the Regions (DETR) launched a strategy, *Building a Better Quality of Life*, in partnership with industry bodies. The strategy's action plan focused on ways to promote a profitable and competitive construction industry in the UK, whilst enhancing and protecting the natural environment. It suggested key themes for action by the construction industry:

- Design for minimum waste
- Lean construction (& minimising waste)
- Minimise energy in construction & use
- Do not pollute
- Enhance biodiversity
- Conserve water resources
- Respect people and local environment
- Set targets (i.e. monitor & report, in order to benchmark performance)

(DTI, 2003a)

Sustainable Construction is a relatively novel idea for the construction industry. A holistic approach to Sustainable Construction involves the integration of economic, social and environmental issues into policy-making.

In economic terms, SC refers to:

- Building a more productive and profitable industry
- Addressing the fragmentation of the construction industry
- Developing and strengthening supply chains and partnering

- Building a more locally based industry to counter the volatility of the economy[1]
- Identifying business opportunities and innovative schemes to address forth-coming EU legislation
- Create the demand for recycled materials

In social terms:
- Building design and tailoring buildings according to the occupiers' needs
- Training
- Health and Safety
- Equal opportunities and the inclusion of women in a male-dominated sector

In environmental terms:
- Improving the overall environmental performance of the industry in its operation (logistics, source materials used locally, use of renewable materials)
- Resource efficiency and reducing waste (waste minimisation, segregation and recycling).
- Improving the environmental performance of buildings, particularly reducing carbon dioxide emissions.

One way to look at the promotion of Sustainable Construction is through the role of the public sector in driving the sector. This is particularly relevant in Wales, given the importance of the construction sector in the Welsh economy and considering the Assembly's commitment to foster Sustainable Development.

The Potential Leading Role of the Public Sector in Driving Sustainable Construction

It is important to note the key role played by the public sector in the promotion of the construction industry in Wales which can be described as a state-run economy: 40 percent of the construction expenditure is initiated by the public sector which accounts for £1.5 billion in Wales annually.

---

1 Today 5-6 major international companies lead the market

Table 4.1. Absolute and Percentage Changes in Output and Orders by Sector

	Output Actual change (£m 1995 prices)	% change	New Orders Actual change (£m 1995 prices)	% change
Public New Housing	199	17.4	72	8.2
Private New Housing	486	7.8	320	7.4
Infrastructure New Work	675	11.0	50	1.0
Public Other New Work	1,023	24.6	618	18.8
Private Industrial New Work	-288	-8.9	-387	-16.8
Private Commercial New Work	1,178	11.1	504	6.1
Public Housing R&M	-171	-3.4		
Private Housing R&M	408	4.6		
Public Non-Housing R&M	439	9.2		
Private Non-Housing R&M	501	5.7		
Total	4,450	7.5	1,179	4.9

(DTI, 2003b).

Figures have been rounded

Table 4.2. Absolute and Percentage Changes in Both Output and New Orders for Each Region in 2002

	Output Actual change (£m current)	% change	New Orders Actual change (£m current)	% change
Scotland	-41	-0.6	63	2.3
North East	345	15.2	130	12.6
North West	1,033	15.1	724	27.5
Yorkshire & the Humber	669	12.6	360	17.4
East Midlands	1,034	25.1	433	26.4
West Midlands	193	2.7	-630	-18.9
Wales	**352**	**14.4**	**264**	**27.4**
South West	1,355	24.2	622	27.9
East of England	779	10.8	386	13.3
London	1,964	17.0	365	6.4
South East	630	5.6	-305	-7.4
Total	**8,312**	**11.8**	**2,412**	**8.2**

(DTI, 2003b). Figures have been rounded

These tables are indicative of the crucial role that the public sector plays in the development of the construction industry in Wales[2] . Table 4.1 shows that new orders in most sectors grew in the year to the third quarter of 2002, with only private industrial new work showing a fall. Public non-housing orders grew the fastest and also showed the largest actual increase. Public non-housing new work[3] was also the fastest growing output sector, although in absolute terms, private commercial new work showed a larger increase. Not only is the construction industry a major contributor to the Welsh economy, it is also an important employer and plays a crucial role in the social and environmental development of the country.

---

2 Although Table 4.1 gives UK-wide figures which are not specific to Wales, it still provides an indication of the role played by the public sector in the industry.

3 Non housing New Work covers activities such as oil installations, furnaces, coke oven and other buildings, coal mine construction and the like. For full details see DTI, 2003b.

While the public sector is clearly a key stakeholder in promoting Sustainable Construction, this is not to say that the private sector should not be encouraged to develop programmes and practices. The role of the policy-maker is to find ways in which both the public and private sectors can be directed in helping the construction industry along this route.

The Difficulty in Designing Policy Guidance for the Welsh Construction Sector

Profile of the Welsh Construction Sector

The position of the construction sector[4] in Wales is considerable: in 2001, the DTI's annual construction statistics report pointed out that the Welsh construction market comprises 7916 private contracting firms. The construction industry in Wales, like that for other parts of the UK, is marked by the prevalence of SMEs. With 6010 (or 76%) of those firms comprising 1-3 employees, the sector is dominated by micro-businesses. The Welsh (i.e. those companies having a registered office and a primary trading office in Wales) construction industry as a whole is smaller than that of England in terms of maximum company size. It has no indigenous companies of a very large size (over 1200 employees) whereas England has 51 (0.03% of the total number of English companies). Wales has about 350 medium-sized companies, which accounts for the same proportion of companies in the range 300-1199 employees as England (0.1% of the total). Registered office and trading office data show that there are some 245 construction companies from outside Wales (i.e. from England, Scotland, Northern Ireland, the Republic of Ireland or the British Crown dependencies) that have a trading address in Wales and, of these, 31 have a larger turnover than the largest 'native' Welsh construction company. Assuming that these larger construction companies from outside Wales do actually undertake work in Wales rather than just having a nominal trading address in Wales, it is reasonable to conclude from this latter point that there is a UK-wide construction market, at least as far as the larger companies are concerned, rather than just a Welsh construction market open only to Welsh companies.

---

4   The construction sector is one of the major industrial sectors in the UK: in total, it accounts for 9% of the UK's Gross Domestic Product (GDP). The output of the industry, which has increased by 9.7% from 2001 to 2002, reached £81.9bn in 2002.

Sector Characteristics and Complexity in Defining its Boundaries

One of the difficulties encountered when tackling the construction sector is that it encompasses a wide range of very diverse activities, from the production of building materials, to the design, operation, repair, maintenance and demolition of buildings. The construction sector is a generic term covering a vast array of activities and professions:

- Clients (i.e. people commissioning the building)
- Professional Consultants (architects, engineers, surveyors, project managers etc.)
- Construction companies (contractors, suppliers, manufacturers etc.)

It involves so many different types of actors that there are persisting divisions between different disciplines. Given the multi-disciplinary nature of the sector, it is a challenging task to identify catalyst points to drive the industry and elaborate policies that can be implemented across the board. Furthermore, the diverse nature of the sector makes it difficult to create robust supply chains and to co-ordinate actions amongst stakeholders. An official from the Welsh Development Agency (WDA) has confirmed in an interview that it is more difficult to create a supply chain in the construction sector than in the automotive or food sectors. He pointed out the short-term nature of contracts which give a volatile character to the sector, as supply chains tend to have a short life span. This characteristic of the construction sector demonstrates the difficulty of embarking on business development programmes without a long-term perspective.

Not only is it challenging to design policy guidance for the whole sector in the first place, but the Assembly's constitutional commitment to implement Sustainable Development policies in the exercise of its functions means that policy guidance directed at construction companies operating specifically in Wales should have an even stronger focus on SC than in the UK guidelines as a whole. In that context, one question that the Assembly has to address regards the classification and definition of the boundaries of the construction sector - in terms of types of work and activities - in Wales and whether it encompasses firms with their registered office address in Wales or whether it includes all construction companies working on projects in Wales.

Extent and Limit of the Assembly's Powers to Design Effective Construction Policies

To understand the development of construction policy in Wales it is essential to appreciate the policy context of devolution and the Welsh Assembly Government commitment to promoting sustainable development. Unlike the Scottish Parliament, the Welsh Assembly has no primary legislative powers, and no capacity to vary taxes. Thus, in the context of construction policy, it implies that the Assembly cannot impose more stringent building regulations. Nor can the Assembly initiate financial incentives to drive the market towards the use of recycled materials by increasing the Landfill Tax or Aggregate Levy. In addition, it would not be viable for the Assembly to draw its own regulations or introduce legal or financial instruments that would apply only to Welsh businesses. If, for instance, the Assembly wished to place further producer responsibility obligations by setting more environmentally-orientated construction specification regulation, it would concern only Welsh firms. It would be necessary to place an obligation on any companies operating in Wales. Yet the absence of border control is a real impediment to the practical implementation of such additional measures.

Recent Policy Developments in the Construction Sector in Wales and the UK

WAG Policy Profile: Absence of a Systematic Strategy

Despite the importance of the construction industry in the Welsh economy, the Assembly has not developed a coherent strategy to promote the sector as a whole, taking into consideration the full sustainable construction agenda. First of all, the Assembly's Housing Directorate5 has focused its attention on housing rather than on the construction industry in its entirety. It has produced a housing strategy, *A National Housing Strategy for Wales*. The strategy recognises the principles advocated by the 1998 Egan report "Rethinking Construction" and states key indicators of improvement in performance identified in the "Rethinking Construction Report": 'reduction in capital cost, construction time, defects, accidents; and increases in predictability, productivity, turnover and profits' (NAW, 2001: 86). However, the Welsh Assembly Government has not produced a strategic, target- driven document to lead the sector towards Sustainable Construction or commissioned the Rethinking Construction Centre for Wales to do so.

Secondly, the initiatives[6] put forward by the Welsh Assembly Government's Housing Directorate concentrate on the social and economic aspects of sustainable development rather than the environmental. The key issues are those of public

---

5   There are 70 members of staff in the Assembly's Housing directorate of which 11 work in the Construction and Domestic Energy Branch.

ownership, improvement of training, continuity in partnering and the development of supply chains at the local and regional levels. During an interview, an official has stressed that, apart from the broad drive to improve the quality and efficiency of the construction sector, two major issues that need to be addressed are:

- Training: there is a basic lack of skilled workers and the construction industry has to raise its image in order to attract young people and retain skilled workers within the sector.
- Safety and Health: construction is recognised as one of the most dangerous industries in which to work and it needs to improve its working conditions and safety.

It was also mentioned during the interview that environmental standards for new construction are not the most important priority, as new buildings represent a very small percentage of the existing building stock. Sustainable construction is promoted more in terms of the social and economic benefits it can generate within local communities and in making the industry more attractive to work in. While it is recognised that the social and economic aspects of sustainability are vitally important, a lack of focus on the environment means that significant impacts may not be fully addressed.

The extent to which WAG should drive the construction sector is a key policy-related question. An Assembly official reported that the Assembly's main role is *"to set expectation"* and to facilitate and encourage construction stakeholders to work together. The Assembly has supported the establishment of the Rethinking Construction Centre for Wales as part of its general promotion of Rethinking Construction and construction best practice in Wales. The Centre has a co-ordinating role and is very successful in bringing stakeholders together. The table below gives details of the money allocated by the WAG Construction and Domestic Energy Branch to the Rethinking Construction Centre for Wales.

6   The Assembly is promoting Sustainable Construction through: (1) Pathfinder projects to secure employment and train-
    ing at the local level through construction contracts. (2) Training schemes, partnering and supply chains within the pro-
    curement of housing construction by Housing Stock Transfer schemes; (3) Two Objective One projects to improve the
    management of environmental and business performance by construction SMEs. One project is to develop the con-
    struction supply chain within the Welsh timber industry based on the social housing sector. The other is about business
    development and training support for SMEs and involves a partnership of the Construction Industry Training Board,
    Health and Safety Executive, the Welsh Development Agency and the Rethinking Construction Centre for Wales.

Table 4.3. Budget of the WAG Construction and Domestic Energy Branch to support the promotion of Rethinking Construction

SCHEDULE OF GRANT OFFER	(YR1) 2002-03	(YR2) 2003-04	(YR3) 2004-05	(YR 4) 2005-06
Grant aid to Rethinking Construction Centre for Wales:				
Percentage grant aided	50%	90%	80%	70%
Towards Business Plan Costs	41,500	94,500	97,800	89,740
Towards CPN workshops	0	21,000	21,000	21,000
Total grant aid to Rethinking Construction Centre for Wales	**41,500**	**115,500**	**118,800**	**110,740**
Purchase of Local Govt Task Force promotional material		2,000	2,000	2,000

However, Welsh construction industry representatives expressed their willingness to receive more policy guidance than that currently provided by the Rethinking Construction Centre for Wales. They believe that the Welsh Assembly Government should lead the sector by providing a strategy to guide business support organisations and other construction industry stakeholders. It would be disappointing for the Assembly to miss such an opportunity to become involved in driving Sustainable Development in one key industrial sector in Wales.

Lack of Strategic Guidance and Poorly Coordinated Business Support Network

It is worth noting the difficulty in co-ordinating sustainable construction related policies amongst different divisions within the Welsh Assembly Government and in ensuring that they are addressed in a systematic way. On one hand, WAG can be praised for its effort to promote green procurement across the board. There is a Construction Forum within the Assembly which co-ordinates the work of individual divisions and Assembly agencies to improve procurement procedures, environmental and energy efficiency standards in Assembly funded construction projects. Divisions included in the Forum are:

- Transport
- Education
- Health
- Estates
- Procurement
- Heritage organisations

On the other hand, joint working between Assembly divisions is not systematic and this undermines the implementation of sustainable construction initiatives. No long-term working relationships have been developed so far between the Waste Policy Division, the Housing Directorate and the Sustainable Development team to co-ordinate actions towards the efficient delivery of sustainable construction policies (like the improvement in Construction and Demolition Waste Management, recycling and re-use).

What is more, although there are initiatives that bring together key business support organisations in Wales, they do not have a particular emphasis on tackling environmental issues in the construction sector. For instance, the Welsh Development Agency has a partnership with Arena Network and Groundwork Wales to promote better waste and resource management at the firm level through the Business Environmental Coordinator Programme. The WDA works in collaboration with the Rethinking Construction Centre for Wales but the environmental agenda is not highly developed. In addition neither the WDA nor RCCW seems to have close links with the Waste Resources Action Programme to address C&D waste as a specific issue. For instance, WRAP is working on the promotion of use of recycled aggregates but no synergies or joint projects exist with the Welsh Development Agency to investigate potentials of market for recyclates development. No sub-group has been established in the Wales Waste Forum to tackle that issue, despite the recognition of the need for one in the Welsh waste strategy *Wise About Waste* (WAG, 2002). Moreover, Welsh Regional Waste Planning Groups tend to follow the WAG agenda and so they too have paid little attention to developing an infrastructure for C&D waste. It is doubtful whether policy guidance and voluntary agreements represent sufficiently strong incentives to promote Sustainable Construction and better resource and waste management and to motivate businesses to improve their practices.

Table 4.4. Role of the Welsh Assembly and Assembly Sponsored Public Bodies

ORGANISATIONS	FUNCTION	STRENGTHS	WEAKNESSES
Welsh Assembly Government (WAG)	Design policy to drive the construction sector in Wales.	Constitutional commitment to promote SD	Lack of strong leadership to direct the Sustainable Construction agenda. WAG has delegated all of its responsibility to promote Sustainable Construction to RCCW.
WAG Housing Directorate	Housing Policy	Substantial grant aid to RCCW	No policy guidance aimed at the whole construction sector. Policy guidance focuses on Housing.
WAG Sustainable Development (SD) Team	Ensure WAG policy co-ordination amongst various departments towards the delivery of SD	Recognition of SD as a key issue.	Poorly resourced. Is SD an empty driver? Rhetorical discourse about SD without the necessary commitment to put it into practice.
WAG Waste Policy Division	Waste Policy	Design of extremely comprehensive strategy to address waste issues.	The Welsh waste strategy has given priority to household waste management to the detriment of other waste streams[i]. The former accounts for 6% of total waste produced in Wales whilst C&D reaches 15%.
Rethinking Construction Centre for Wales (RCCW)[ii]	Client leadership & procurement; Innovation & Best Practice; Health & Safety; Skills & Training; Industry Measurement & Monitoring; Sustainable Construction.	Disseminate knowledge and good practices to SMEs about SC and organise regular conferences to improve the sector performance.	Poorly resourced.

i   Although some C&D waste recycling targets have been set in the strategy, senior officials have recognised during an interview that specific arrangement to tackle C&D have yet to be made.

ii The Centre work programme is being set out through Task Groups which are made up of industry representatives. The Board of Management includes representatives from ICE (Wales), RICS, Universities, CITB, CECA, CIC Wales, HSE and Rethinking Construction.

Table 4.4. Role of the Welsh Assembly and Assembly Sponsored Public Bodies (continued)

ORGANISATIONS	FUNCTION	STRENGTHS	WEAKNESSES
The Welsh Development Agency (WDA)	Promote economic development in Wales.	Work with Arena Network waste minimisation programme at company level.	Lack of commitment and expertise to address the needs of the construction sector; absence of focused policy aimed at the sector.
Arena Network	Provide guidance on environmental matters to businesses.	See above, partnership working with another ASPB.	Self-selecting audience. No focused policy guidance for construction companies.
WRAP	Investigate the potential development of markets for recycled materials	Studies carried out on the use of aggregates.	Insufficient working relationships with other stakeholders to design joint strategy.
Wales Waste Forum[i]	Gather waste stakeholders in Wales to address waste policy issues.	Consultative and open approach amongst dedicated stakeholders.	Does not hold a sub-group for Construction and Demolition waste stream.

i   The Wales Waste Forum unites stakeholders from industry, local authorities, higher education, voluntary sector, business support organisations such as the Welsh Development Agency and the Waste as Resource Action Programme which seeks to enhance markets for recyclates, the Environment Agency, trade organisations and businesses involved in waste management.

Although it is recognised that WAG can develop certain policies, it remains constrained by the context in which it works.

Assessment of the Key Policy Instruments Used to Direct the Construction Sector towards Waste Minimisation

Weak Regulatory Measures to Improve the Management of Construction and Demolition Waste

At the outset it is important to consider the nature of the EU legal framework, given the importance of its impact at the Member State level. When looking at EU environmental legislation aimed at promoting sustainable construction, it must be noted that regulation so far has tended to concentrate on end of pipe solutions. It is only recently that the EU has issued a Directive on Energy Performance in Buildings to address issues of resource efficiency upstream and look at the ways in which materials and waste are generated. Thus, this section focuses on Construction and Demolition (C&D) waste management as it provides a good example of the mechanisms used to support sustainable construction at the UK and Welsh levels.

The European Commission has identified a number of priority waste streams because they pose a potential threat to the environment. Inert and C&D waste is one of these. What is rather surprising therefore is that C&D waste is dealt with as part of the EU general approach to waste management, perhaps most notably the Landfill Directive (99/31/EC) rather than as a specific waste stream like Packaging (which has its own Directive 2000/53/EC). The lack of measures targeted at C&D waste may be a significant omission if other measures to reduce and better manage C&D waste are also found wanting. The absence of specific regulation of C&D waste at the European level is mirrored at the UK level. Construction waste related legislation concentrates essentially on the diversion of waste from landfill, largely instigated by the EU Landfill Directive, as well as on the use of secondary aggregates, with the aim of encouraging construction waste segregation, re-use and recycling. The WAG does not have the power to pass primary legislation and so it cannot close this regulatory gap on its own.

Taxes and Market Development

There are two main taxes to promote better waste management and resource productivity in the construction industry in the UK. The Landfill Tax, which was introduced in 1996, and the Aggregates Levy, which came into force in 2002, seek to ensure that material recovery becomes the most competitive solution for waste management, and in turn enhance market opportunities for recyclates. The Landfill Tax has encouraged producers to look for alternative uses for construction waste and has contributed to the diversion of C&D waste from landfill. According to a recent UK Government study (ODPM, 2001), almost half of the C&D wastes produced in England and Wales are re-used or recycled. Out of the total waste stream, more than 38 million tonnes was recycled as aggregate in 2001; compared to 22.7 million tonnes in 1999. Whilst these figures are laudable it is difficult to know how much they should be attributed to the Landfill Tax. The level of the tax for inert waste is far cheaper (£2) than for active waste (£13). At its current level, the tax would not seem to provide a big incentive to minimise C&D waste.

---

7 The Aggregate levy charges £1.60 for every ton of newly quarried materials such as sand and gravel. The chief aims of the levy are to internalise the external environmental costs of aggregate production; to encourage the use of alternative materials and development of new recycling processes; and to promote more efficient use of virgin aggregate.

With regard to the effectiveness of the Aggregates Levy[7] and the new Aggregates Levy Sustainability Fund (ALSF) to address C&D waste management, again the results are mixed. There are isolated examples of C&D waste minimisation and recycling in projects such as the Trent Valley GeoArchaeology study and the Archaeology South East study on Lydd quarry (English Heritage, 2003). The levy has also opened some market opportunities for companies that can use recycled aggregates in their activities. For instance, RMC has reduced its operational cost by using recycled green glass as road building materials.

However, a study for the Office of the Deputy Prime Minister (ODPM) has pointed out that there are limits to market development for C&D waste. One of the study's findings was that the 'scope for further recycling of C&D waste for use outside landfills and registered exempt sites appear to be limited by the fact that much of the C&D waste that was not being recycled as aggregate was not physically capable of forming aggregate, because it was wholly or largely made up of soil' (ODPM, 2001).

Novel instruments for environmental protection appear to be meeting significant challenges in promoting better management of C&D waste. Once again the WAG finds itself at a disadvantage in seeking to overcome any shortcomings as it has no powers over taxation.

Voluntary initiatives

At the industry level, there is a wide range of best practice cases which provide advice on aspects of the management of C&D waste including the reduction of construction waste, waste segregation and re-use as well as the use of secondary aggregates. For instance, the Building Research Establishment (BRE) has launched a construction waste material exchange scheme on the internet; the Construction Industry Research and Information Association (CIRIA) provides a database of construction-related recycling facilities in Great Britain that accept or sell materials and promote localised recycling of materials. These kinds of initiatives provide incentives for construction companies to engage in recycling activities as there are clear cost savings to be gained from reduced costs for waste disposal, reduced landfill taxes and transportation costs.

The Department of the Environment, Transport and the Regions launched in April 2000 a strategy for sustainable construction *Building a Better Quality of Life* that sets out some clear targets to improve the construction industry's building practices. Resource efficiency is recognised as a fundamental element and the strategy underlines the importance of *"designing for minimum waste"* and *"re-using existing built assets"*. The Office of Government Commerce has adopted an action plan, *Achieving Sustainability in Construction Procurement* (OGC, 2003), so that the public sector can become a leader and exemplar in green procurement in construction by promoting the use of materials with low environmental impact or made from renewable resources. All UK government departments agreed to implement the action plan by March 2003. As government procurement accounts for 40% by value of the UK construction market, the public sector plays a key role in the promotion of resource productivity and waste minimisation. The specifying of recycled and reclaimed materials in tender documents will encourage the segregation and recovery of materials. The strategy was developed in partnership with industry bodies, and may have been unduly sympathetic to business interests as it places no direct requirements on clients or suppliers of building materials to use environmentally friendly materials or to improve their C&D waste management.

Table 4.5. Incentives and Initiatives for Waste Minimisation in the Construction Sector

Type of incentive	English and Welsh initiatives	Welsh initiatives
Waste minimisation guidance	CIRIA, Construction Industry Research and Information Association The Construction Confederation, DTI, Department of Trade and Industry Construction Best Practice Programme	Edexcel training courses (partnership between Environment Agency, Fforwm, Groundwork Wales, Penarth Management Consultants) Business and Environment Challenge Scheme
Waste recovery and recycling support	CIRIA reclaimed and recycled construction materials handbook BRE internet Materials Information Exchange Government's Aggregates Information Service (AIS) WRAP Waste as Resources Action Programme	Objective 1 and 2 Fund projects: the Centre for Research In the Built Environment project Arena Network waste exchange
Transport efficiency	CIRIA recycling sites map (materials recovery and recycling)	
Planning Guidance	PPG45 for England only	Minerals Planning Policy Wales Technical Advice Note TAN 21 on Waste

As Table 4.5 shows, there are a plethora of initiatives in place in England and Wales to tackle C&D wastes, from waste minimisation programmes to re-use and recycling guidance. Yet, current support programmes tend to operate independently of each other and there seems to be little co-ordination among stakeholders. Two points are important to note here.

First, it has proved notoriously difficult to promote improved environmental practices amongst SMEs and so a sector dominated by such firms is likely to have a poor record in dealing with its wastes. Market differentiation leads firms to engage in different types of construction projects and this may well affect the way in which they manage their waste. It is usual in the construction sector for the larger companies to seek to win work on the larger and more complex projects where there is less competition from the smaller companies and where their competitive advantage lies in their expertise and capitalisation. Thus, Welsh companies operating in Wales are in effect constrained in the actual Welsh construction market (i.e. one that is open to competition from non-home Welsh companies) to either obtaining work as members of the larger companies' supply chains or bidding for smaller scale local projects.

Second, although the Welsh waste strategy is weak on policy guidance for C&D waste, it should be noted that the Assembly Government has dedicated some Objective 1 and 2 Funds specifically to support the implementation of waste recycling and re-use activities in the construction sector. For instance, the Centre for Research in the Built Environment (CRIBE) seeks to raise awareness of best waste management practices in construction SMEs. In its quest to divert C&D waste from landfill and to promote markets for recyclates, the Assembly Government is looking at the way in which this kind of initiative could be mainstreamed throughout Wales.

Learning from good practice: The Case of the Netherlands

Background to Sustainable Construction in the Netherlands

The 'best practice' visit carried out under the OSKaR project has demonstrated that the Netherlands has a more focused and wide-ranging approach to the promotion of sustainable construction than that currently being pursued in Wales. Environmental issues generally, and in relation to the activities of the construction industry in particular, have a higher priority in the Netherlands than in Wales.

This is due to the relatively small size of the country and the demands of increasing population, economic activities, mobility and quality of life aspirations, constrained by climate change, land subsidence, a rise in sea levels and the ever-present threat of sea-inundation. The need to rebuild large areas of the country after the Second World

War led to the creation of CUR (the Netherlands Centre for Civil Engineering Research and Codes), an organisation that is now seen as the hub of a network of practitioners seeking to generate and disseminate knowledge for a sustainable society. CUR was established in 1952 as a community of practice of knowledge workers focusing on research and development for building materials and new, fast and cheap construction methods embedded in a quality assured infrastructure. There are now around 3000 individual members of the network (CURnet) with around 15 national and international collaborative research projects being undertaken at the present time. It is seen as an independent voice of the construction industry and as a public-private partnership. It focuses on pre-competitive knowledge management with an emphasis on both process (i.e. acting as a learning community) and on product (e.g. handbooks, guides textbooks etc.).

Concern about the environmental aspects of construction seems to have been high on the political agenda since at least the mid-eighties but sustainability from the holistic point of view (i.e. incorporating economic and social considerations as well as environmental), is however a fairly new concept in Holland. It was in the early 1990s that the Dutch took a particular interest in 'sustainability' in a holistic way, and the business case and social aspects of environmentally-conscious buildings were considered in many development projects. In addition, open competition and the desire to have a positive environmental business image drove SMEs towards innovative ideas. However, the concept of partnership was found to be one of the main sources of innovation and communication within and between SMEs. For economic growth, it was necessary to include SMEs in the supply chain of many large construction groups.

Innovative work on recycling activities and energy efficient buildings led to the concept of recycling and waste segregation being very advanced, but in the late 1990s, it was observed that compliance with environmental legislation was affecting productivity and product costs thereby having an unacceptable economic cost. In other words this focus on environmental compliance had tended to overshadow the economic impact assessment of initiatives. As a result, under recent legislation, the Dutch government is reducing the legal requirements for environmentally-conscious building design and process.

Nevertheless there is still a strong focus on the environmental aspects of sustainability which is being led by a specially appointed government agency, Novem. Novem is the Netherlands Agency for Energy and the Environment. Its mission is to stimulate sustainable development within society with regard to energy and the environment both within the Netherlands and abroad. It is an agency of the Ministry of Economic Affairs and has some 425 employees. Its identity is of an organisation that is passionate for sustainable development and its core business is the delivery of government programmes as an intermediary between the government and the market. Its targets for 2010 are to achieve a reduction of 60% in the use of fossil fuels in the operation of new buildings and of 25% in the existing building stock; a reduction of 20% in the use of 'A' quality water in buildings; a reduction of 20% in the use of materials in the construction of buildings (associated with environmental performance standards for new build houses); 99% re-use of construction and demolition waste (currently said to be 85%); and a reduction of 50% in the amount of household waste produced. Novem's scope of activities includes: sustainable building, sustainable production, sustainable energy and sustainable transport.

As with CUR, it appears that the use of the term 'sustainable' in the dealings that Novem has with the construction industry is well understood. Given that it is a government-sponsored agency, it is possible to criticise Novem's approach to the promotion of sustainability as being typically bureaucratic and 'top down'. The impression gained, however, was that it provided the necessary robust framework (backed by government policy and legislation) of advice and support within which effective knowledge dissemination can happen and effective action promoted and encouraged.

Demonstration Projects

Novem felt that demonstration projects provided a useful way of disseminating information about best practice. The conversion of best practice building operations into legal and policy requirements by the Dutch Government was one of the key ways in which this new agenda was communicated to SMEs. However, these policy and other legal requirements were not simply imposed on SMEs; they were developed in conjunction with stakeholders from across the construction industry as a whole. This approach reduced resistance from building professionals to changes brought about by policy and legislation.

One such demonstration project that exhibits the full range of issues arising in sustainable construction is an urban regeneration development of sheltered apartments and associated community facilities in Zevenaar for people aged over 50. The project has been designed for a life of 75 years, rather than the more usual 50 years reflecting a whole-life cost best practice in economic sustainability. It was designed on the so-called 'open construction' process, allowing for both individual and local community participation in the design of the overall development and of the individual apartments which were tailored to the initial tenants' wishes using a full size mock-up in a local community centre. The development comprises some 169 independent apartments and a sheltered nucleus of 49 units providing additional care for older residents if and when they may need it, thereby enabling them to remain in the complex for the remainder of their lives if they so wish and hence addressing social sustainability issues in an innovative way.

The development also incorporates a number of interesting environmental innovations for a development of this type including the use of an earth and sedum covered roof for its insulation and rainwater storage properties, and an extensive range of environmentally sound construction materials such as:

- Construction concrete and concrete tile featuring 20% recycled concrete granulate;
- Natural gypsum for sprayed-plasterwork ceilings;
- A high percentage of shell lime in the cement mortar;
- Use of timber from cultivated sources and naturally resistant red cedar for exterior applications;
- Sand-lime bricks for load-bearing walls;
- Double-glazed red cedar window frames with special ventilating sections throughout;
- Mineral wool insulation;
- Natural paint with a linseed oil and natural resin base.

Construction waste was also separated on site allowing for increased re-use of materials and easier recycling at waste disposal facilities. The disposal of construction and demolition waste has become a significant industry in the Netherlands now as a result of stringent targets for recycling having been established, the banning of all recyclable and combustible material from landfill and the use of high levels of landfill tax. Waste management companies have been able to exploit this situation in collaboration with the construction industry to the extent that the use of recyclates in construction processes is now common, subject of course to meeting the necessary specifications.

The construction process at the Pelgromhof Project, Zevenaar also featured strong partnership relationships between the main contractor and his suppliers and between the client, the architect and the contractor.

This project demonstrated what can be achieved by an enlightened client, in this case a charitable foundation, in delivering a construction project that fully recognises the breadth of meanings associated with the concept of sustainability. It was felt that although this development was an outstanding example of this approach it was not that unusual in the Netherlands.

There seem to be three important features to the apparent success of the process of implementing sustainable construction in the Netherlands. Firstly, there is the age-old polder (literally a piece of land reclaimed from the sea) culture. This creates a common and clearly understood commitment to the primary and fundamental need to ensure that the country was secure from environmental threat (originally, of course, from the sea but now for example from increasing population and an increased risk of flooding from climate change) before the processes of business development were allowed to operate. This has meant that the concept of sustainable development and indeed sustainable construction is well understood in the Netherlands and these concepts appeared to be an integral part of the normal discourse of everyone that the visit party met from the construction industry there. Notwithstanding the recent balancing of economic with environmental objectives in the Netherlands there is still a strong emphasis on the need further to improve the environmental performance of the industry and the infrastructure that it creates.

Secondly, the process is strongly influenced by the strategic and policy framework that has been established by the national and provincial governments, supported by a government-funded agency tasked with the delivery of target-driven improvements to the performance of the built environment. The Novem agency established in 1975 has a key role as an intermediary between the government and the market and hence, like CUR, has developed a long-standing credibility as the supporter of sustainable construction.

Thirdly, the integrated provision of advice and guidance to both developers and constructors appears to be crucial. This information creation and knowledge dissemination dimension to the process needs to be based on a robust understanding of the particular needs of the construction industry as it confronts the changing world of sustainability. Traditionally it is an industry dominated by micro-businesses or SMEs with pressing day-to-day concerns of cash flow and survival. They have limited, if any, spare resources available to address what they may perceive as unnecessary and expensive burdens to their businesses. Whilst the larger companies are progressive in their understanding of the emerging issues they are requiring members of their supply chains to be fully up to speed with the new agenda. It is the responsibility both of the SMEs themselves and the providers of publicly-funded business support services to ensure that knowledge of sustainable construction becomes an integral part of the construction industry as a whole.

Transferability of Good Practice

To achieve and promote good practice for sustainability, it is important that it should be viewed from a three dimensional perspective. Sustainability cannot be achieved by promoting or complying with environmental aspects only - all compliance and initiatives have to make economic sense. The Netherlands experience shows that considering environmental aspects only has affected productivity and time efficiency, and consequently it has affected business viability.

For any development, it is necessary to investigate the impact of the development on local or regional economic strategies. It should include the assessment of whole-life costing on the design criteria, as well as its impact on time and the overall cost of the project. It is also necessary to assess the impact on overall development plans of the region. Stakeholders should be included in development pre-design and design stages.

In terms of environmental policies and introduction of any sustainability indicators, it is necessary to promote the infrastructure for it, e.g. waste segregation and minimisation requires adequate facilities for sorting and recycling facilities. It can also be promoted by looking at market diffusion. The business case of all newly introduced initiatives should be assessed.

Sustainability is of great importance to both the building industry and to society as a whole. The building sector consumes more than 50% of natural resources, produces more than 50% of waste from its operations and consumes more than 40% of energy in Europe. In order to achieve sustainability in construction, a holistic approach is required that incorporates environmental consciousness, economic competitiveness and social inclusion.

It is important to recognise that sustainability in the built environment has a regional perspective. For example, the industry might be sustainable in one particular region but not in others. This could manifest itself through differences in the availability of resources between regions, or variations in technological demands or social behaviour between regions. In this way, criteria of sustainability can vary from region to region. However, lessons can be learned and technology or process can be transferred with regional modifications. Thus, in terms of eco-efficiency, best practice approaches can be transferred between regions.

The TASK programme as a whole is concerned with processes of creating and disseminating knowledge about sustainability, so as to make progress towards a sustainable knowledge-based region. This 'region' is comprised not only of people as individuals and communities but also as employees of a large number of SMEs. A significant number of these in Wales are in the construction sector. It is important therefore that these businesses should be enabled to become aware of the issues of sustainability as they affect their activities both immediately and in the future. 'Sustainable construction', covering the triple bottom line concerns of sustainability for the sector, could be an effective shorthand phrase around which to structure discussions about the future of physical infrastructure development in Wales. Sustainability as a concept seems to be understood more widely in the construction industry in the Netherlands than it is in Wales. This may be because concerns about the environment have featured more significantly over a longer period of time there than here (although the Aberfan Coal Tip disaster in 1966, in which 144 people died, focused attention on the issue of landform instability in Wales at the time).

The real question for Wales, however, and it is a question for the Assembly Government to address as a matter of priority if it is serious about sustainable development, is how to avoid the 50 years (at least) that the Netherlands has been thinking about and discussing (and thereby creating knowledge about) the environmental implications of construction. Clearly a first step in this process, following the example of the Netherlands, is to establish a dialogue with all those who have an interest in the role that an environmentally aware and high performing construction industry plays in sustainable economic and social development in Wales.

Conclusion and Recommendations

This chapter has explored issues surrounding the promotion of sustainability within the construction industry. The construction sector plays a major role in Wales by providing both employment and the essential physical infrastructure for the processes of economic and social development. However, considerable environmental impacts arise from its activities in both the construction phase itself (e.g. in the production of C&D waste) and from the long term operation of the constructed facilities (e.g. from CO_2 emissions from buildings) and the use of transport infrastructure.

Given its constitutional requirement to promote sustainable development, the Welsh Assembly Government has a duty to promote the sustainability of the construction industry and limit its environmental impacts as much as possible. The Assembly requires an understanding of the economic pressures that lead to wasteful and environmentally neglectful actions by the industry. Two main factors explain this phenomenon: firstly, such situations can be attributed to the current market-oriented and short-term financial evaluation perspective adopted by clients in both the private and public sectors for construction facilities. In addition, there is a lack of committed leadership by the Welsh Assembly Government to enhance sustainable construction in Wales.

A business case can be and has been made for sustainable construction: it is based essentially on taking a long term view (for example through the use of whole-life costing techniques) of each project. The public sector has a key role to play in this approach as it is the client for an estimated 40% of the construction market, and publicly-funded initiatives directed at improving the performance of the industry abound. The latest of these initiatives is Rethinking Construction which was established following the publication of the report of the same name by the then Construction Task Force under the chairmanship of Sir John Egan in 1998. Whilst the focus of the initiative has been very much on general improvements in the performance of construction companies, an additional aim has recently been added, the need to address sustainability issues in the industry, following the launch in 2000 of the UK Government's strategy for sustainable construction – Building a Better Quality of Life.

However, the full implementation of this strategy has been hampered by a lack of clarity about its applicability to Wales following devolution. This difficulty has been compounded by two further factors: on one hand, responsibilities between the UK Government and the Assembly for the management of the implementation of the Rethinking Construction initiative in Wales are ill-defined. Whilst there has been a 'regionalisation' process for the initiative that led to the establishment of the Rethinking Construction Centre for Wales in 2002, there is still a lack of clarity about whether it is a UK- wide initiative with leadership by, and accountability to, the DTI in London or whether the Assembly Government is responsible for deciding how it is implemented in Wales. The RCCW was established with funding assistance from the Assembly Government but its remit has been constrained to merely coordinating an externally determined programme of activities rather than the development of something more specific to Wales, based on a rigorous analysis of the issues in Wales, not least the Assembly's duty to pursue sustainable development. On the other hand, the nature of the construction market in Wales contributes to explain why it is difficult to change practices at the Welsh level. The construction sector is dominated by SMEs that operate mostly as sub-contractors; thus they have little influence over the whole business operation process and their activities are dependent on the demand of main contractors which do not necessarily integrate sustainability specifications in their construction project.

The best practice visit to the Netherlands demonstrated the impact that solid government leadership, together with practical industry-led support, can have in defining the terms within which the construction market develops. A sophisticated policy framework is clearly of crucial importance in allowing markets to develop taking into account all aspects of sustainable construction.

Such government leadership of the sustainable construction agenda seems to be lacking in Wales so far. This was the strong message that came from construction industry representatives who took part in a seminar organised by the RCCW Sustainable Construction Task Group in May 2003, focusing on the development of a Sustainable Construction Action Plan for Wales. The current review of the effectiveness of the Assembly Government's Sustainable Development Scheme provides a timely opportunity to address this leadership deficit through various actions.

Recommendations:

- Establish a Strategic Forum for Construction for Wales, comprising both client and constructor representatives, assertively led by the Assembly Government to develop a Sustainable Construction Action Plan for Wales that should include the full range of concerns i.e. the social and economic dimensions of sustainability as well as the environmental. This plan should also include proposals to address the need for 'green' infrastructure projects for both community and economic development and should recognise that the question of ownership of physical assets (e.g. through housing stock transfer initiatives) can enable innovative construction procurement processes (oriented more firmly to community benefit) to be introduced (e.g. through the Welsh Procurement Initiative);

- Acknowledgement in the revised WAG Sustainable Development Scheme of the key role that construction and physical infrastructure development play in the future prosperity of Wales and the quality of life of its inhabitants;

- Undertake a thorough analysis of the construction sector in Wales including a review of the existing sustainability performance of the industry (both its environmental and social performance) from the perspective of both clients and constructors,

- Establish a Construction Industry Measurement and Monitoring capability in Wales able to review overall past performance, to examine economic development opportunities associated with the industry (e.g. the use of Welsh timber and off-site manufacture of components) and to forecast future requirements of the industry (for example, for skills in particular occupations);

- Undertake a review of the existing business support services for the construction industry in Wales, possibly leading to the transfer of the (extended) responsibilities of the Rethinking Construction Centre for Wales to the WDA (as is the situation in Scotland). This would allow for a more focused approach to the provision of support, for example through the support for localised supply chains based on highly developed environmental performance of the individual companies;

- Empower the WDA so that it becomes the reference body for advice on the Welsh construction sector. RCCW should be part of the WDA and become a catalyst forum to drive forward the Assembly's agenda for change.

References

Cohen, C., Flynn, A. and Ryder, J. (2003) 'Waste Policy in Wales: The Case of Construction and Demolition' in Dhir, R.K., Newlands, M.D. and Dyer, T.D. (eds) *Sustainable Waste Management*, Thomas Telford Publishing, London, 2003, pp 95-104.

DEFRA (2003) *Energy and Environmental Management*, Department of Environment, Food and Rural Affairs

DETR (2000) *Building a better quality of life*, Department of the Environment, Transport and the Regions

DTI (2003a) http://www.dti.gov.uk/construction/sustain/scb.pdf, Department of Trade and Industry

DTI (2003b) http://www.dti.gov.uk/construction/stats/constat2003.pdf, Department of Trade and Industry

English Heritage (2003) http://www.english-heritage.org.uk

National Assembly for Wales (2001) *Better Homes for People in Wales, A National Housing Strategy for Wales.*

National Assembly for Wales (2003) *A Winning Wales - the National Economic Development Strategy of the Welsh Assembly Government, annual report 2002-2003*

Office of the Deputy Prime Minister (2001) *Survey of Arisings and Use of Construction and Demolition Waste in England and Wales in 2001.* www.planning.odpm.gov.uk/

Office of Government Commerce (2003) http://www.ogc.gov.uk

Welsh Assembly Government (2002) *Wise About Waste: The National Waste Strategy for Wales*, June 2002.

Chapter 5

Implementing an Integrated and Sustainable Waste Strategy: Scope, Challenges and Opportunities for Wales

Caroline Cohen

Introduction

Faced with the problems of environmental degradation, non-renewable resource depletion and climate change, the European Union (EU) has put forward a series of Environmental Action Programmes (EAPs) to address environmental protection. They are a mark of the institutionalisation of environmental policy at the European level and its integration into public policies in Member State countries. One of the key concerns of EU environmental policy is to address the sustainability of economic development. Waste growth appears as one of the most difficult and important issues and the Sixth Environment Action Programme, *Environment 2010: Our Future, Our Choice*, calls for significant improvement in the domains of waste prevention and management. It seeks to meet this objective through improved resource efficiency, a shift to more sustainable production and consumption patterns and waste initiatives.

It is important to appreciate the policy context in which waste policy develops at the UK and Welsh levels. First, the advent of a European environmental policy framework has had a major impact on waste policy implementation and process in the United Kingdom (UK). More than flagging up the country's endemic 'implementation deficit', it has fuelled a new approach to waste management which is now recognised as a critical issue to be addressed. *The Waste Strategy 2000 for England and Wales*, published by the Department for the Environment, Transport and the Regions (DETR) reflects EU policy aims and objectives and follows the EU agenda to deal with different waste streams. Second, the development of waste policy at UK and Welsh levels has to be understood within the context of *multi-level governance* characterised by a multi-layered power structure encompassing local, regional, national and supra-national levels of government. The devolution agenda has had a major impact on waste policy-making. New responsibilities have been allocated to British regions and led to the development of regional waste management strategies. Wales has developed its own approach to waste management policy, in accordance with the EU agenda. This chapter provides an overview of the scope, challenge and opportunities associated with the implementation of the strategy. Great emphasis will be put on the crucial drivers and the role and powers of various actors from the public, voluntary and private sectors to promote sustainable waste management practices.

Waste has been recognised as "Wales' biggest environmental problem" by the Welsh Assembly First Minister, Rt.Hon Rhodri Morgan AM, and the former Minister for the Environment, Sue Essex AM. With around 23 million tonnes of waste produced each year in Wales, of which 42% is buried into the ground, the country has a long way to go to develop a more sustainable waste management system. This would involve the development of recycling facilities dealing with a wide range of waste streams[1]. The traditional over reliance on landfill as a disposal route is especially significant for municipal waste[2] and the Welsh Assembly Government (WAG) has recently put great effort into developing an integrated approach to tackle these issues. It published its own National Waste Strategy, *Wise about Waste* in June 2002, which advocates a cultural shift in waste management towards more sustainable practices in all realms of society, involving householders, the public sector and industry. One of the key issues for policy stakeholders at EU, UK and Welsh levels is to combine sustained economic growth with environmental protection, i.e. to achieve a decoupling of resource use from economic growth and limit waste production, which currently grows on average by 3 per cent each year whilst the annual rate of growth in the UK in the second quarter of 2003 reached 2 per cent and Wales Gross Value Added (GVA) for 2001 was 3.9 per cent (National Statistics, 2003).

The allocation of power in the waste related domain at the regional level entails two kinds of policy development:

• *Capacity Building*; the region's empowerment strongly depends on its ability to explore new policy options and develop competence in waste management. Thus, institutional learning is likely to involve target setting, organisational change and introducing new policy instruments whilst taking into consideration good practice elsewhere and the locality's characteristics.

---

1   Waste streams include Agricultural Waste, Hazardous Waste, Construction and Demolition (C&D) waste, Electrical and Electronic Equipment, End-of-Life Vehicles, Composting, Glass, Metal, Tyres and so on. For full details, see http://www.wasteguide.org.uk/
2   In 2001, 92% of municipal waste was disposed in landfill in Wales.

• *Integration*; regions have to undertake a holistic approach to waste management based on policy co-ordination and partnership, both horizontally, i.e. within the geographical area and vertically, amongst bodies at EU and UK levels. These tiers of government often have very different approaches to waste management and the region has to seek to influence policy-making at both UK and EU levels.

The waste strategy is at an early stage of implementation and waste stakeholders in Wales are still exploring best practice schemes which exist at the European, UK and Welsh levels to gain an insight into appropriate methods that can be implemented in accordance with the region's needs and attributes. With 76% of its waste diverted from landfill, the Netherlands appear as a leader in sustainable waste management in Europe and a best practice visit was organised there to investigate the transferability of both sustainable waste policies and practices to the Welsh region. Thanks to the best practice visit organised by the OSKaR project, it was possible to have an in depth look at a successful waste management model in Europe and to evaluate the potential applications of the Dutch model to Wales in view of developing market opportunities.

The chapter seeks to evaluate the performance of the Welsh Assembly Government in implementing better waste management practices, given its constitutional requirements to generate and integrate Sustainable Development (SD) into the policies it develops in the exercise of its functions. First of all, the chapter gives an extensive definition of the realm of SD in the waste sector and provides an overview of the way in which the SD agenda is taken forward at the Welsh level. Second, it stresses the leadership role of the Assembly in bringing sustainable waste management to the fore in Wales and assesses the extent and limit of its success, given its power constraints. It then looks at the way in which the Assembly engages and interacts with key stakeholders to meet its waste strategy targets and outlines some policy implementation problems. Third, it outlines the outcomes of a best practice visit carried out in the Netherlands with an emphasis on the scope and challenges associated with sustainable waste policies and transferability of practices. It considers how knowledge of sustainable waste management is disseminated through different types of business networks and evaluates whether the organisational structure that exists in Wales enables strategic and operational goals and targets to be achieved. Some conclusions and recommendations are then presented.

The Challenges of Developing a Sustainable Waste Strategy

The development of sustainable waste policies has to be understood in the context of ecological modernisation, which is a key paradigm advocated in the EU to reconcile and combine economic growth with environmental protection (European Commission, 1993). In order to get a good understanding of the responsibilities of the Welsh Assembly Government, it is important to outline the key elements of sustainability in the waste domain. Its waste strategy seeks to encompass and integrate environmental, economic and social issues into policy-making.

The environmental dimension can be summarised by the waste hierarchy as shown in Table 5.1 below, which prioritises waste management options according to their environmental impact.

Table 5.1. The Waste Hierarchy

WASTE REDUCTION
–
RE-USE
–
COMPOSTING – RECYCLING
–
ENERGY FROM WASTE
–
LANDFILL

It must be noted that although waste prevention comes at the top of the waste hierarchy, policy-makers have not concentrated their attention on that matter and hardly any instruments have been developed to foster waste minimisation. In policy terms, decoupling environmental degradation from economic growth involves the development of a dual strategy based on sustainable production and consumption. Improvement in eco-design - which focuses on the life cycle of a product and its environmental impact - is key to resource efficiency and waste reduction. Yet, so far, little action has been taken to develop an Integrated Product Policy (IPP) and little attention has been paid to the respective roles of businesses and consumers (ENDS, 2003). At the implementation level, the waste hierarchy raises the question of the type of facilities to be created to move away from landfilling. Despite public objection to the proliferation of waste treatment sites, forthcoming EC legislation entails the development of new infrastructures for the adequate treatment of specific waste streams and their associated long-term cost. It is worth noting that in contrast to other European countries, there is a strong opposition to incineration as a waste treatment method in Wales. Although local authorities tend to favour the development of recycling facilities on existing landfill sites, further location points have to be identified for the creation of facilities.

In economic terms, one of the key challenges of a regional strategy is to create the necessary incentives to ensure that material recovery (including material reprocessing and recycling) becomes the most competitive solution for waste management, whilst having limited control over legislation and taxation. It is questionable whether Wales has the necessary power to deliver its strategic waste objectives, as the main policy instruments used to promote better waste management are determined by central government and apply to both England and Wales. Many stakeholders have pointed out the weakness of the policy instruments: the level of the landfill tax and aggregate levy is far too low to send the right signals to businesses and stimulate the necessary change in their waste management practices, such as waste segregation. In the UK, the landfill tax current level attains €19 or £14 per tonne for active waste and €3 or £2 per tonne for inert waste; in contrast, the Netherlands has introduced stringent taxation level: €120 or £84 per tonne for combustible waste and €70 or £49 per tonne for non-combustible waste. Landfill is still the cheapest disposal option and the tax fails to create a sufficient incentive to encourage better waste management and the creation of markets for recyclates, or foster the development of adequate waste facilities for the treatments of various waste streams. Given these power constraints, the Assembly's difficult tasks are to identify where market opportunities lie and to develop alternative and innovative schemes that address specific waste streams. Furthermore, in order to ensure the economic viability of the strategy, the Assembly seeks to provide the necessary support to businesses to create and stabilise markets for recyclates and to strengthen the supply chain To that end, the Assembly fosters its working relationships with key organisations involved in the development of efficient waste markets such as the Waste as Resources Action Programme (WRAP) and the Wales Environmental Trust (WET). Moreover, the Assembly can play a potentially pivotal role in strengthening the economy through the promotion of green procurement – the purchasing of recycled and environmentally friendly materials and equipment – across the whole public sector.

The Assembly seeks to cultivate joint working amongst neighbouring local authorities on plans and funds in order to create the demand for recycled materials and realise economies of scale. To further that aim, the WAG has awarded financial support to a private company to convert the Shotton Paper newsprint mill, located in North Wales, into a 100 per cent recycled fibre pulp facility.

From a social perspective, the Welsh strategy seeks to engage the community as much as possible for three main reasons. First of all, community involvement and participation in better waste management practices are more likely to encourage a change in people's culture and attitude to waste. The British are often portrayed as "the dirty men of Europe" and there is a need to commit people to improve the quality of their local environment. It can be argued that local residents have the tendency to project responsibilities onto the Council and the perception that it is the local authority's duty to tackle waste issues. Second, it has to create a sense of ownership based on accountability, transparency and inclusiveness. In other words, the public must be consulted and involved in the process so that it participates in decision-making regarding the waste activities and infrastructure being developed. Local authorities have to gain public support for the types of waste facilities they wish to implement and find the most adequate ones according to the characteristics and needs of the given locality. Third, the waste strategy has a strong community element as there is a potential to create jobs through community based recycling groups. Currently, the voluntary sector involved in waste management activities in Wales employs more than 300 people. They undertake a wide range of initiatives such as kerbside collection, the management of civic amenity sites, furniture recycling and nappies schemes, recycling of electrical and electronic equipment as well as textiles.

The Assembly Leadership, Current Policy Development and Problems

The Welsh Assembly Government advocates a cultural shift in waste practices in all realms of society and has recently made great efforts in developing an integrated approach amongst stakeholders. The waste strategy recognises that the development of a sustainable waste management system in Wales can bring about economic, social and environmental opportunities. This section looks at the powers held by the National Assembly for Wales (NAW) and the WAG to develop waste policies; it also looks at the Assembly's relationship with key actors from the public, voluntary and private sectors and their respective roles in waste policy implementation; current policy problems are then outlined.

A Strong Commitment From the Assembly: Powers and Vision

In order to assess the extent to which waste management can be improved in Wales, it is important to look at the powers held by the Assembly to make and implement its own policies. To understand the development of waste policy in Wales, it is essential to appreciate the policy context of devolution and the Assembly's commitment to promoting sustainable development. A major challenge for the WAG is that

"it does not control some of the crucial levers required to make a fundamental change in the way waste is managed in Wales" (WAG, 2002a).

Unlike the Scottish Parliament, the NAW has neither primary legislative nor tax varying powers. For instance, the WAG does not have the constitutional right to introduce or amend primary legislation and is unable to vary the level of landfill tax or introduce variable charging for household waste collection. Furthermore, it is very limited in its ability to apply producer responsibility initiatives in Wales, due to the unrestricted movement of products across the English-Welsh border. So the WAG finds itself in a highly dependent situation as it recognises:

"for a number of the Assembly Government's aspirations to be delivered, action has to be taken in conjunction with UK Government" (WAG, 2002b).

Nevertheless, the Assembly's policy remits are wide ranging and to describe it as a "glorified County Council" is to underestimate its significance seriously. From a legislative perspective, under section 93 of the Environment Act 1995, the NAW has the power to make regulations to further waste minimisation and promote the re-use, recovery or recycling of materials (NAW, 2001). Moreover, under section 121 of the Government of Wales Act 1998, there is bestowed on the Assembly a responsibility for sustainable development that is unique for an elected body in Britain. The section states that

"The Assembly shall make a scheme setting out how it proposes, in the exercise of its functions, to promote sustainable development".

The one set of relationships where the WAG can exercise some authority is with regard to local government and so, not surprisingly, many of the targets and actions are aimed at local authorities who emerge as key partners in the Welsh strategy. An illustration of the WAG's power can be seen in the much more stringent recycling and composting targets it has set in its waste strategy *Wise About Waste* (WAG,2002b) compared with those established in the *Waste Strategy 2000* for England and Wales[3]. The extent of the WAG's power can also be appreciated from a budgetary standpoint. The Assembly is in control of its own significant budget and has allocated considerable additional funding to local government for it to meet the municipal waste targets: £79m is being shared out evenly among local authorities for the period 2001-02/2004-05 according to the Standard Spending Assessment formula, a means of calculating Rate Support Grant to local authorities, taking into account the demographic and geographic characteristics of the authority. Here it is worth noting that contrary to the situation in England, the waste budget allocated to local authorities is ring-fenced and set up for three years. This compares with a one year funding system in England where the waste budget is allocated on a competitive basis and is not ring-fenced. It can be argued that thanks to the policies developed at the Welsh Assembly level, Welsh local authorities are given greater means to improve their waste practices and thus are in a much more favourable position to meet the national targets than their English counterparts.

The Assembly's strong commitment to promote and facilitate better waste management practices across the board can be analysed through four main levers identified in Table 5.2. The table shows that the Assembly provides much stronger support to the public and voluntary sectors than to the private sector and this is in large part a reflection of where it can exercise influence.

---

3   The latter sets a target of at least 25% of household waste recycling or composting by 2005, 30% by 2010 and 33% by 2015. The former seeks to achieve at least 25% recycling/composting of municipal waste (rather than household waste) with a minimum of 10% composting (with only compost derived from source segregated materials counting) and 10% recycling by 2006/07 and achieve at least 40% recycling/composting by 2009/10 with a minimum of 15% composting and 15% recycling (WAG, 2002).

Table 5.2. The WAG's Waste Change Instruments

Assembly's Levers / Partners	Funding	Policy Guidance	Audit	Awareness Raising
Local Authorities	Substantial capital support	Comprehensive	Regular and methodical	Consistent problem oriented
Voluntary Sector	Grant aid	Strongly promoting involvement, yet vague on substance	Regular	Regular
Private Sector	Indirect assistance, looking for easy wins	Unsystematic, not targeted at waste companies	Partial, selective through IPPC legislation	Uneven and ad hoc
Higher Education	Variety of projects through LTCS, Objective 1, 2 and 3 and WAG	Avoiding duplication of work and sharing of resources	Variable	Regular

i. Partnership Working Relationship Between Regional and Local Government.

The Assembly's levers aimed at local government are highly developed: the support to local authorities is based on substantial funding for the development of more sustainable waste practices, the production of the waste strategy for Wales and guidance on the design of municipal waste management strategies. Besides, great effort has been made to improve municipal waste data which is key to the effective operation of strategic waste policies. Thanks to more accurate data collection and monitoring, key waste streams can be identified and in turn, the planning of the necessary infrastructure can be developed. The Assembly is also very supportive of local authorities vis-à-vis unforeseen and upcoming issues (such as abandoned vehicles, composting of animal by-products) and organises meetings when necessary.

ii. Openness of the WAG to the Direct Involvement of the Voluntary and Community Sectors

In its quest to foster a partnership approach between local government and the voluntary sector, the Assembly seeks to promote a robust involvement of community groups in the implementation of the strategy and is funding a number of recycling schemes. It is worth noting the flexible style that the Assembly has adopted with the voluntary sector. The Assembly has regular interactions/contacts with partners involving progress reports, yet it leaves recycling groups a lot of leeway to deliver the strategy set targets. One key pilot project currently under way is the *High Diversion Exemplar Projects* set up by Cylch - Wales' umbrella organisation for community recycling groups - in partnership with the Welsh Local Government Association (WLGA) and the Welsh Assembly Government. Each of the five projects are based on a working relationship between the local authority and the community recycling sector to deliver recycling services to their communities (mostly through kerbside collection, the separate collection and treatment of various waste streams, repair and re-use systems). The idea of this initiative is to demonstrate that regardless of their starting point, whether they are located in rural or urban areas, local authorities with very different waste performance levels can successfully divert 50% of their municipal waste from landfill within three years by adopting an effective recycling system[4]. The Assembly seeks to disseminate and transfer the lessons learnt from these pilot projects to other local authorities in order to mainstream good practice. However, this venture has been criticised by stakeholders from exemplar and non exemplar local authorities for having an exclusive focus on kerbside collection which is the sole recycling method being put forward; some local authorities which did not tender for this project complained that a "one size fits all" approach was not appropriate. They stressed the lack of support for alternative initiatives to kerbside collection, which does not coincide with the street design of their locality. Moreover, some people interviewed pointed out that tensions amongst partners have occurred in exemplar local authorities where the role and responsibilities of each stakeholder was not clearly defined.

iii. A More Cautious Relationship with the Waste Industry

The WDA's report on Environmental Goods and Services (EGS) indicates a major growth of the waste management sector in Wales over the last six years which is mostly attributed to government's targets to increase recycling (WDA, 2002). The report

---

4   The selected local authorities for the Exemplar Projects are Anglesey, Ceredigion, Powys, Torfaen and Newport. Funding was sought from New Opportunities Fund (NOF), Landfill Tax Credit System (LTCS), Objective 1, 2 and 3.

shows that the number of companies in the waste sector has more than tripled over the last five years, from 75 in 1997 to more than 230 in 2002 and respectively employment grew from about 2000 workers to about 5000 (WDA, 2002). Major developments in waste activities occurred in the sphere of waste collection and disposal markets as well as reprocessing and re-use. The Assembly provides indirect assistance to the waste sector5 : for instance, it offers support to Welsh waste businesses via the sponsorship of business support organisations such as Arena Network, Groundwork, the Welsh Development Agency and the Green Dragon programme. Yet, it seems that policy guidance to businesses is turned towards eco-efficiency rather than a structured and thorough analysis of market development opportunities; the approach is rather reactive and based on tackling the most pressing issue (such as the treatment of hazardous waste). It is true that the Assembly engages with waste companies and related trade organisations to explore options for the treatment and disposal of specific waste streams that are subject to considerable market and regulatory changes6, subsequent to recent and forthcoming EC legislation. However, more strategic thinking and integration are needed to move away from end of pipe solutions and investigate innovative approaches to recycling and opportunities for market development. Interviews with various stakeholder revealed that there is too little communication between those organisations aiming to support businesses such as WRAP and WET and those charged with waste collection and disposal or those involved in technical and market management activities. Thus, the potential combination of different types of recycled and segregated materials for re-use is not fully considered.

iv. Towards a Co-ordinated Relationship Between Academia and Key Stakeholders

Although higher education is not identified as a key partner in the strategy, The Assembly recognises the crucial role that Research and Development (R&D) plays in waste policy effectiveness and it has developed good links with universities and academics across Wales. The Assembly contributes to the funding of a wide range of research projects. One funded project worth mentioning is the Wales Centre of Excellence for Waste Research (WCEWR) which is to develop a systematic and integrated network amongst waste stakeholders from both the public and private sectors. More than simply bringing together funding for research in Wales and co-ordinating research teams from Welsh universities and colleges to avoid duplication of work, the

---

5   The case of Shotton Paper Mill mentioned in the introduction reveals the difficulty of getting EC permission for government assistance to industry, especially as EC rules tend to prevent direct state aid to industry (http://www.wrap.org.uk/).
6   Waste streams such as Hazardous waste, Electrical and Electronic Equipment, Plastic, Compost.

Centre has the potential to link together various research initiatives involving researchers, industry practitioners, policy-makers and the voluntary sector in connection with the national waste strategy for Wales, *Wise About Waste*. Its catalyst role could be conducive to greater coherence and effectiveness of the waste management sector in Wales.

Current policy problems

i. A Focus on Municipal Waste to the Detriment of Other Waste Streams

It can be argued that the Welsh Assembly's policy approach has a bias towards the treatment of municipal waste to the detriment of other waste streams. As Table 5.3 indicates, Municipal Waste accounts for less than 6% of the total waste produced in Wales, compared with Construction and Demolition Waste, for instance, which nearly reaches 15%. Of course, municipal waste is a pressing issue in Wales as its management has historically been characterised by an over-reliance on landfill as a disposal route as shown in Table 5.4. A key question that arises is to determine which waste streams need most attention, according to its impact on the environment. Consideration must be given to the "Best Practicable Environmental Option" (BPEO)[7] for managing different types of waste in different localities. It should be noted that there is very limited information available on the sources and fates of waste in Wales and it is not feasible to give an accurate breakdown of the types and origins of the waste landfilled. Also, no reliable figures exist for the amount of commercial and industrial waste which is recycled. This points to the problem of waste data collection and monitoring in the private sector: there is a lack of statutory requirements to promote firms' waste segregation and data provision especially with regard to SMEs at the UK level, which is mirrored at the Welsh level.

---

7   In some circumstances landfill may indeed be the BPEO.

Table 5.3. Waste Production in Wales and England[†] (1998-99)
Quantity produced (tonnes per annum)

Waste streams	England & Wales	%	Rank	England	%	Rank	Wales*	%	Rank
Industrial	51,920,000	12.5	4	46,931,000	11.9	4	4,989,000	21.5	3
Commercial	23,600,000	5.7	6	22,459,000	5.7	7	1,141,000	5	6
Municipal	28,320,000	6.9	5	26,990,000	6.9	6	1,330,000	5.7	5
C&D	70,800,000	17	3	67,515,000	17.2	3	3,285,000	14.1	4
Mines and Quarries	118,000,000	28.4	1	112,000,000	28.6	1	6,000,000	25.8	2
Sewage Sludge	28,320,000	6.9	5	27,915,000	7.2	5	405,000	1.7	7
Agricultural	94,400,000	22.6	2	88,325,000	22.5	2	6,075,000	26.2	1
TOTAL	415,360,000	100		392,135,000	100		23,225,000	100	

(Environment Agency, 2003)

† (1) Dredging waste has been excluded from the table because figures are only available for England and Wales; (2) C&D stands for Construction and Demolition waste.

Table 5.4. Waste Management Methods Used for Different Types of Waste in Wales in 1998/99
(000s tonnes)

Waste Land Disposal and Treatment Method / Waste Streams[i]	Land Disposal	Land Recovery	Re-used	Recycled	Thermal	Transfer	Treatment	Un-recorded	Total
Industrial	1,650	17	1,478	1,574	34	8	210	20	4,989
Commercial	781	5	19	182	3	50	31	71	1,141
Municipal	1,262			69[ii]					1,331

(Environment Agency, 2003) Figures have been rounded

i Industrial and Commercial wastes both include: Inert Construction and Demolition wastes, paper & card, general industrial and commercial, other general and biodegradable, metal and scrap equipment, contaminated wastes, mineral wastes and residues, chemical and other. See website for more details.
ii The figures do not give the breakdown of composting and recycling levels.

An important caveat to the data in the table above relates to its quality. It is difficult to provide accurate waste data in terms of waste streams and waste treatment methods. Municipal waste data collection is becoming systematic but that is not the case for commercial and industrial waste and figures remain approximate.

ii. Mismatch Between the Assembly's Power and Aspirations?

Although the strategy gives considerable importance to decoupling resource use and waste production from economic growth, the Assembly has not developed the policies and the necessary policy instruments to meet its policy objectives. There is no policy within the strategy which has a direct focus on the promotion of eco-design or resource efficiency which would foster waste minimisation. As a result, composting, re-use and recycling practices prevail over waste prevention. Business support organisations such as Arena Network and the Welsh Development Agency provide "independent advice on practical ways to minimise waste and convert turnover into profit" (NAW, 2004) However, improvement in waste management at the firm level remains highly dependent on the willingness of the company itself to join such voluntary programmes. With regard to the public sector, the Assembly requires local authorities to meet composting and recycling targets, thus they do not prioritise waste minimisation and there are no incentives for them to go beyond the set targets. Local authorities concentrate on tangibles which can be measured in quantitative terms such as tonnes of waste being recycled[8] .

iii. Planning for Waste: Providing the Right Facilities in the Right Places.

The development planning system has a key role to play in ensuring the establishment of an integrated network of disposal installations in the region. Currently, there is no large scale transfer station/recycling centre to manage the municipal waste collected by local authorities in Wales. There are no hazardous waste treatment facilities and the recycling plants dealing with various waste streams such as Construction and Demolition Waste or Electric and Electronic Equipment are of a minor scale. Key issues which need to be considered include the development of an adequate infrastructure for recycling and the improvement of waste data collection, especially in the private sector, as these are fundamental to achieving the effective operation of strategic waste policies. Local authorities seek to undertake recycling activities on existing landfill sites as much as possible, yet it is recognised that to meet EU waste policy goals, additional land is needed beyond that currently committed. It is worth noting that the Welsh waste strategy has led to greater co-ordination amongst

---

8   Recycling is weight rather than material driven.

local authorities for waste planning. Four years ago, local authorities used to plan for the provision of land for waste management facilities in isolation from one another. Although there is no formal requirement to work jointly with neighbouring local authorities, the setting up of three regional waste groups will help meet EU principles of regional self-sufficiency in waste disposal and the proximity of waste facilities to the source of the waste. Another pressing issue is the degree of involvement and responsibility of businesses in the management and development of the necessary infrastructure for the treatment of special waste. During interviews, WAG officials have stressed the difficulty of engaging with manufacturers and retailers on planning matters. Despite the WAG's willingness and effort to consult the private sector over the regional waste plans, only a small proportion of businesses responded, mostly from organisations directly involved in the collection and disposal of various waste streams.

Best Practice and Policy Transfer: From the Netherlands to Wales

During the Best Practice Visit to the Netherlands - a country renowned for being at the forefront of sustainable waste management - a number of sites dealing with specific waste streams were visited[9]. It is worth bringing to attention some examples of the management of various types of waste that are carried out there, as these sorts of facilities will need to be developed in Wales over the next decade. The three private companies presented below respectively deal with Waste Electrical and Electronic Equipment (WEEE), hazardous waste and plastic recycling.

Table 5.5. Coolrec, Waste Electrical and Electronic Equipment (WEEE) Recycling Facility

Main Activity	Dismantles domestic electrical appliances for recycling and disposal (mostly fridges and TV).
Operation	The recycling fee levied by manufacturers on the purchase price is used to fund the company's activity.

9   Facilities visited included a transfer station for municipal waste management, a WEEE recycling facility, a Construction & Demolition waste material recovery site, hazardous waste facilities, composting plants and a plastic recycling firm. For full details, see Sustainable Regions, Volume 2, Issue 1, Cardiff Business School, 2003.

Table 5.5. Coolrec, Waste Electrical and Electronic Equipment (WEEE) Recycling Facility (continued)

Drawbacks of the Dutch system	There is no incentive from a flat fee levy to encourage manufacturers to design their product for recyclability. A take-back scheme system or the collection of goods the manufacturers produced are more conducive to eco-efficiency.
Application to Wales	Although WEEE plants operate in Wales, dismantling facilities of this kind need to be developed to meet and go beyond the requirements of the recent EC WEEE Directive. Such plants will have to be funded directly, or collectively, by the EEE manufacturers and retailers. Representatives of one of the major EEE manufacturers in Wales have already visited the plant in Rotterdam (Cohen, Downes and Rees, 2003).

Table 5.6. ATM (Shanks) Hazardous Waste Treatment Facility (Thermal and Biological)

Three Main Waste Treatment Processes	The Thermal Soil Purification Installation treats soil, rubble and other materials contaminated with organic pollutants such as oil and cyanide. The pyrolysis installation processes organic waste materials in solid and sludge form. The industrial wastewater biological treatment plant treats organic wastewaters and sludges.
Public Relations	An open door policy with neighbouring communities is in practice, yet the company does not publish monitoring results widely other than in an annual environmental report. The company sponsors community activities and employs 200 staff.
Application to Wales	One controversial issue regards the potential development of hazardous waste treatment plants and their locations, given the public reluctance to their development. This raises the question of preventing and minimising the use of hazardous materials in production processes. Until this point is addressed, there is a need to develop hazardous waste treatment plants for the foreseeable future. Plants thermally treating organic wastes, and meeting strict environmentally protective emission standards, will provide part of the answer (Cohen, Downes and Rees, 2003).

Table 5.7. Lankhorst Recycled Plastic Products Manufacturing Plant.

Main Activity	Produces high quality thick walled plastic products, (including fencing, decking, street furniture, manhole chambers, boarding, bollards, pipe carriers), most of which are made from recyclates. Processes and recycles plastic film used for silage. It operates a patented 'intrusion' process that is a mix of traditional extrusion and injection technologies.
Barriers to growth	In the Netherlands: - Poor perception of secondary material / virgin material. - Cost; other material like wood is cheaper on the market. - Reprocessability; Improving technical "know-how". - High initial investments and economies of scale for the business to be viable.	In Wales: - Lack of sustained competitive pricing for recyclates /virgin polymers. Creating the demand. - Poor collection of materials. - Quality control of feedstock. - Testing capacity issues. - Limited investment in R&D to improve the efficiency reprocessors. - Standards and specifications.
Application to Wales	This is the kind of facility that needs to be developed in Wales to bring sustainable development to the fore, ensuring that there are locally based factories making products from recycled plastic sourced in Wales and from the rest of the UK. Much of this is beyond the direct control of the Assembly Government – the breaking down of many of the barriers and the use of various levers to open up the markets for recycled products are largely in the hands of UK government (e.g. through raw materials taxes, tax incentives, etc). The Assembly Government can, however, encourage the public sector in Wales to procure products made from recycled materials (e.g. in this case, traffic cones, bollards, park benches, fencing etc all made from recycled plastic) (Cohen, Downes and Rees, 2003).

Strengths of the Dutch Waste Policy Model: What Are the Lessons for Wales?

It is important to outline where the strengths of the Dutch waste management policy system lie. Three important points which set the context for waste management should be noted. First, given the geography of the country, there is limited opportunity for landfill: this is due to the country's low altitude level, which combined with a high population density have severely restricted the land available for landfill. Second, the social, political and economic circumstances of the country seem to be more conducive to stakeholders' consensus on the principles and content of waste policy. In Britain, there is a strong wish to accelerate the rate of economic growth and promote societal renewal, whilst in the Netherlands there is a more explicit recognition of the need to manage the impacts of industry and consumers on the environment. This may also explain why the Netherlands is more inclined to engage in a fundamental review about the long term direction of waste policy. Third, the success of the Netherlands' policy is also based on a holistic and systematic approach to waste management, where the instruments used are wide-ranging and well co-ordinated with one another. The Dutch Ministry of Housing, Spatial Planning and the Environment (VROM) has adopted a dual strategy which combines tight regulatory measures with strong economic and financial instruments (these points are developed in the following paragraphs).

i. A Strong Political Will From Central Government

The Dutch Ministry of Housing, Spatial Planning and the Environment can be praised for its pro-active approach to waste management and setting challenging waste targets. In 2001, it drew up a National Waste Management Plan in conjunction with the Waste Management Council (representing the three tiers of Government in the Netherlands: national, provincial and municipal) that determines waste policy for the following four years. The Plan seeks to ensure that the proportion of waste applied for useful purposes rises from just over 76% in 2002 to 83% by 2012. A target of 60% has also been set for the recycling of household waste for 2000 and 80% for 2010. Thanks to central government's commitment, more than 74% of total waste was reused or recycled in 1997.

Table 5.8. Patterns of Waste Disposal/Treatment Methods in the Netherlands

Waste Disposal/ Treatment Methods	(%)
Recycling	70[i]
Recovery	9
Incineration	13
Landfill	8
Total	100

(VROM, 2003).

i   Of which 46% is household waste.

The table shows that the Netherlands has a diversified disposal strategy which relies mostly on recycling, compared with Wales which is still dependent on landfill. Municipal waste recycling and composting rates in Wales are, however, set to rise substantially over the next seven years principally as a result of additional specific grant funding from the Assembly Government, and the setting of targets which are monitored as local authority Performance Indicators. Thus, Wales can learn from Dutch recycling practices and transfer some successful schemes.

The cornerstone for household waste recycling in the Netherlands is separation of recyclables at source (i.e. by the householder). The Environmental Management Act 1993 requires local authorities to carry out separate collection of kitchen and garden waste (which make up around 50% of the household waste stream in the Netherlands). This is in advance of, and in accordance with, the likely direction that the forthcoming EC Biowaste Directive will take. Provincial environmental ordinances require local authorities to arrange for the collection of paper, cardboard, glass, textiles and small-scale chemical waste separated at source. Furthermore, municipalities can make a charge for collection and some do so, on the basis of variable charging according to the amount collected.

With regard to industrial and commercial waste, the Dutch Environmental Management Act 1993 requires that waste that cannot be prevented must be separated into different waste streams, kept separately, and transferred separately, if reasonably practicable. This enables it to be re-used and recycled, rather than incinerated or land-filled. There is no such stringent legislation in the UK, however it is possible that Article 6 of the Landfill Directive which requires pre-treatment of all waste prior to landfill may provide the impetus needed for businesses to substantially increase the amount of source separation, recycling and recovery. This point stresses the importance of legislation to drive changes in waste management practices at Welsh and to a wider extent, UK levels.

ii. A Robust Regulatory Framework

A major asset of the Dutch waste policy framework is that it involves the participation of the general public as much as businesses. The concept of producer responsibility is fully comprehensive, as separation at source is a legal requirement for both commercial and industrial waste as well as for household waste. Moreover, the wastes dumped in landfill sites are limited to those which cannot be recycled or incinerated. A total of 35 waste types are banned from landfill; this compares with the United Kingdom where most of household waste ends up in landfill without being treated. In order to ensure the smooth enforcement of the regulation, a practical monitoring system has been put in place. "Waste officers" employed by local authorities are in charge of checking whether householders have completed their recycling duty by segregating their waste and are entitled to charge free-riders. Similarly, regular checks are carried out at the firm level by the environmental regulatory body. A high landfill tax, together with mandatory requirements for the source separation of household, industrial and commercial wastes, have led to high rates of recycling, composting and energy from waste, and a very low rate of landfill (Cohen, Downes and Rees, 2003).

iii. A Set of Co-ordinated Financial Instruments

The main financial incentive for the reduction of industrial and commercial waste is the landfill tax introduced in 1996, whose cost has risen sharply. By setting such a high level tax, recycling and other waste treatment methods are made more attractive. Material recovery becomes the most competitive solution for waste management, and in turn enhances market opportunities for recyclates. In Wales, as in the rest of the UK, the Landfill Tax has, to date, been set at too low a rate to have a marked influence on waste management. It remains to be seen whether the planned increase in the Landfill Tax to £35 per tonne will have the desired impact on behaviour, in the absence of other policy instruments being brought to bear.

Furthermore, a tax is levied on waste delivered to incinerators to ensure that the waste hierarchy is respected and that environmentally friendly solutions are given a priority. There is not such coherency in taxation at the UK level: there is no energy from waste tax in place and currently, energy from waste plants dealing with mixed waste are exempted from the Climate Change Levy.

With regard to household waste, variable charging is in place in some municipalities. Other incentives encourage recycling through refundable deposit schemes and the purchase of energy efficient domestic appliances through a grant system. Since 2001 the total production of household waste has not increased in the Netherlands and the amount of coarse domestic waste (bulky waste of households) in particular has dropped. This indicates that various producer responsibility initiatives, source separation and recycling/composting are having some effect on the amount of waste discarded by householders. Herman Huisman from the Waste Management Council has stressed that

"there is much debate on the efficiency of variable charging. One might conclude that the only applicable system of variable charging in large cities is the expensive bag. In rural areas, other systems might work. The system on the number of persons/hectare has no effect on waste supply".

iv. An integrated approach involving durable relationship with the private sector.

There is a specific Dutch approach to policy-making that places high regard on consensus and partnerships with industry. The Dutch Government and industry have seen the potential of new markets arising from environmental regulation and have actively sought to position themselves to benefit from new legislation. The country has developed specific policies and promoted voluntary initiatives to address each waste stream, from batteries, to electrical and electronic equipment, to car tyres. With regards to end-of-life vehicles, for instance, VROM set up a processing scheme well before the End of Life Vehicles Directive 2000/53/EC came into force. In 1993, the Auto Recycling Nederland was drawn up in conjunction with the automobile industry, distributors, shredders and dismantlers in order to ensure the recycling of old cars. These kinds of initiatives provide incentives for businesses to engage in recycling activities as there are clear cost savings to be gained. By 1999, some 280,000 cars reached the end of their life and about 86% of the materials in those cars were recycled. The development of such schemes also deters fly-tipping practices from taking place (VROM, 2003).

Potential for Transferability

There are key similarities in the two systems: both countries have a laudable attitude to waste management. For instance, Wales has set higher municipal recycling and composting targets than England and its strategy is more comprehensive than the

Waste Strategy 2000 document for England and Wales. In the Netherlands, the Waste Management Council drew up in January 2001 the 'Stimulation Programme on the Separation and Prevention of Household Waste' which comprises monitoring, benchmarking and communication, including the practical exchange of know-how between municipalities. The Wales "Exemplars Project" seems to be the closest analogy to this initiative. The five local authority partnerships have set themselves a challenge to exceed the 2010 recycling and composting target of 40% by 2006. The results of their endeavours will provide a good practice 'route map' for other Welsh local authorities to follow. Wales has also developed voluntary initiatives for the promotion of sustainable waste management. Interestingly, whilst Wales has engaged strongly with the community sector to promote sustainable waste management practices, waste facilities are mostly owned by the Dutch government (83%) and the community sector does not seem to have any sort of involvement in waste activities.

Wales is at an early stage of sustainable waste management policy development and implementation and the Dutch model could have some positive impact on the future waste strategy for Wales. The best practice visit to the Netherlands was extremely informative in terms of the variety of sites visited and the ability to access the knowledge and experience of government policy makers and stakeholder organisations. The information gathered will be useful when the Wales waste strategy is reviewed in a few years time.

Conclusion and Recommendations

Impact of the Welsh Sustainable Agenda on Waste Management

What difference has the devolution process entailed in waste management at the regional level and to what extent does devolution promote sustainable development? The results are promising but remain mixed so far: this can be attributed to the legal and financial constraints of the Welsh Assembly Government but also to the lack of an indigenous Welsh agenda to address environmental issues in a systematic way.

In environmental terms, two points can be made. It is difficult to provide an accurate estimation of the changes which have occurred in the working practices of businesses, to know how far Wales has reduced its ecological footprint by adopting better waste management practices or to comment on the sustainability of the jobs created in the waste field. However, Wales is committed to reducing its waste management environmental impact and landfilling has lessened, whilst recycling practices have risen sharply over the last few years and will continue to grow. The question of the development of hazardous waste treatment plants is still pending but it is most likely that such facilities will develop in Wales. What is more, Integrated Product Policy needs further attention and the appropriate policy instruments -financial, voluntary and legal – have to be combined adequately to encourage manufacturers to design eco-efficient products which are easy to recycle and dispose of.

In economic terms, the Welsh sustainable waste management agenda has definitely led to job creation both directly within the waste sector with the taking up of sustainable waste management activities, but also indirectly through the provision of the necessary equipment for recycling and composting. Although the initial stimulus is EU-led, Wales distinguishes itself by involving actively the voluntary sector and community groups into the implementation of better waste management practices and this has enabled the employment of many disadvantaged people. Another positive point is the potential leadership role that the public sector could play in promoting green procurement and creating the demand for recycled materials; this could have a major impact on the development of markets for recyclates in Wales and more widely at the UK level. The difficulty lies in having a "joined-up" approach throughout the public sector and in co-ordinating the operation of various departments and public organisations. Besides, as previously stated, the Welsh Assembly has limited power to decouple waste production from economic growth. What kind of policy instruments can it develop to achieve policy goals without adding cost to businesses and local authorities? In other words, what kind of policy incentives can be put in place at the Welsh level so that recycling becomes a cheaper option than landfilling? As direct state aid to industry is difficult, the devolved administration has to flag up its policy objectives to UK and EU levels whilst strengthening its relationship with businesses to find appropriate solutions and direct firms as much as it can with the help of business support groups such as WRAP and the WDA.

From a social perspective, no genuinely Welsh environmental awareness raising campaign has been developed to promote cultural and attitudinal changes in waste practices. Despite a transparent and consultative approach taken by the Assembly, a clearer message must be sent to householders and businesses, perhaps by building up a more focused marketing strategy.

Crucial Drivers for Policy Development and Implementation at the Welsh level

The competence and strong policy leadership from the Waste Policy Division of the Welsh Assembly Government as well the National Assembly for Wales' commitment to promote better waste management practices have contributed to improve both policies and implementation. Thanks to a good institutional structure based on policy guidance, consultation as well as financial support involving substantial grant aid to local authorities and a ring-fenced system, waste management has improved greatly in Wales over the last three years (these elements can be seen as the concrete manifestation of the vigour of the SD agenda). As a result of a number of interviews with stakeholders, it is clear that devolution together with the motivation of key individuals play a central role in waste policy-making and account for much of the recent policy improvement. The role of waste management companies[10] is not to be discarded, yet they tend to communicate with central government rather than the devolved administrations when it comes to policy matters. Some voluntary organisations such as Cylch have also succeeded in helping to shape policies and practices in Wales.

However, it seems that the political culture of Wales can be an impediment to policy changes. Cultural inertia can be seen both within the public sector and the Assembly Government relationship with the private sector. On one hand, the lack of a consensual and integrated approach and "joined-up thinking" amongst various departments within the Assembly and amongst various public sector organisations slow down progress in waste management and policy delivery. The difficulty of mainstreaming green procurement across the public sector in a relatively small geographical area is a good illustration of the weaknesses of the country's political ethos. The Wales waste strategy and related guidance documents seek to promote a cultural change in working practices of the public sector. Despite policy guidance, it proves difficult to enhance local authorities' joint working. For instance, the "Guidance on Municipal Waste Management Strategies in Wales" states that

> "It is imperative that local authorities enter into partnerships with key stakeholders to deliver sustainable waste management. Partners include the community and voluntary sectors, the private sector and other local authorities" (WAG, section 6.1.5, 2002a).

On the other hand, the hesitant relationship that the Welsh Assembly Government has towards the private sector prevents innovative waste management schemes from materialising. Although WAG and businesses share a common understanding of the impact of EU environmental legislation on business practices and the remits of sustainable waste management, they do not work together enough to design joint strategies and find solutions that would work to their mutual advantage. It is important to further the development and activities of the Wales Waste Forum[11] so that actors (from industry, the voluntary sector, government and Assembly Sponsored Public

---

10 Biffa, for instance, has produced an extremely useful document "Future Perfect" which gives an analysis of Britain's waste production and disposal account and states the implications for industry and government for the next twenty years.

Bodies) co-ordinate their actions to ensure the smooth implementation of forthcoming legislation and create innovative schemes for market development. Current support and initiatives tend to operate independently of each other. When interviewed and asked about the way in which the Wales Waste Forum could be a vehicle for policy improvement and co-ordination, one official suggested the creation of subgroups within the forum to address specific waste streams and issues such as hazardous waste, fly-tipping, education and awareness raising. Such changes in the organisational infrastructure would strengthen stakeholders' working relationships and be conducive to the development of market for recyclates. Similarly, it would help green procurement to thrive through public-private partnership voluntary initiatives.

Recommendations

Waste Prevention   Eco-design should be given more attention to reduce initial generation of waste.

Regulation to date has tended to focus on end of pipe. Waste licensing tends to focus on companies handling waste once discarded. Relatively little attention is given through the regulatory system to waste producers. Innovative approaches to promote waste minimisation need to address issues upstream where waste is generated.

Design clear waste minimisation targets to ensure that the waste hierarchy is respected and works at its best and that sustainable treatment methods prevail upon less environmentally friendly ones.

Planning   Improve industrial and commercial waste data collection as these are fundamental to achieving the effective operation of strategic waste policies. There is a lack of accurate data on specific waste streams and a need to trace their source, composition, growth rates, and life cycles. Considerable improvements need to be achieved

---

11 The Wales Waste Forum unites stakeholders from industry, local authorities, higher education, voluntary sector, business support organisations such as the Welsh Development Agency and the Waste as Resource Action Programme which seeks to enhance markets for recyclates, the Environment Agency, trade organisations and businesses involved in waste management.

with SMEs and companies which do not come under IPPC rule.

Strengthen the working relationship of the 3 Regional Waste Groups to plan for the necessary infrastructure to deal with specific waste streams including hazardous waste.

Cultural Change   Ensuring that sustainability issues are the bedrock of waste management requires a wholesale cultural change for individuals, households, businesses and public bodies. There is an urgent need to develop more comprehensive awareness raising and information on waste management practices and options.

Innovative Policy Instruments   Create incentives to ensure that material recovery becomes the most competitive solution for waste management such as:
- rewards schemes to promote eco-design
- consider introducing reduced VAT on eco-labelled products

Integration   To overcome the lack of "horizontal" co-ordination, i.e. amongst stakeholders within the given geographical areas:
Adopt a holistic and systematic approach to waste management throughout the public sector so that it becomes a leader in sustainable waste management and foster the demand for recycled materials through green procurement.

Co-ordinate recycling initiatives amongst local authorities and mainstream best practice projects in order to create markets for recyclates and supply chains on a long term basis.

Improve the connection or communication between business support organisations and organisations charged with dealing with waste disposal. Thus the need to enhance public-private partnership via the Wales Waste Forum to (i) solve current problems of policy implementation related to waste disposal and treatment and (ii) design innovative initiatives conducive to market development.

Develop eco-industrial parks and the necessary infrastructure to organise markets for recyclates with the adequate logistical management of transfer of wastes from point of generation to point of recycling.

Cultivate a working relationship with other partners from the voluntary sector and Higher Education.

There is a lack of "vertical" co-ordination, i.e. amongst institutional bodies at EU, UK and Welsh levels[12]. Ensure that Wales becomes an exemplar in waste management for other English regions given its experience of devolution. In that way, the Assembly will gain influence over policy-making at both UK and European levels.

References

Biffa (2002), *Future Perfect: An Analysis of Britain's Waste Production and Disposal Account,* November 2002.

Cohen, C., Downes and Rees, A. (2003) "Waste Management: Drivers and Outcomes of the Best Practice Visit to the Netherlands", in *Sustainable Regions*, Volume 2, Issue 1, Cardiff Business School, pp 13-16.

Cohen, C., Hines, F. and Lee, R. (2003) *The Future Of Waste Management: Moving Up The Waste Hierarchy.* A submission to the Environment, Food & Rural Affairs (EFRA) Committee by the Centre for Business Relationships, Accountability, Sustainability and Society (BRASS), January 2003.

DETR (2000) *Waste Strategy 2000 for England and Wales,* May 2000, Department of Environment, Transport and the Regions

Environmental Data Services Ltd (2003) The ENDS Report (2003) *Call for New Body to Champion Product Policy*

Environment Agency (2003) http://www.environment-agency.gov.uk/

European Commission (1993) White Paper: "*Growth, Competitiveness, Employment*", Brussels.

---

12 However, this characterisation does not apply between WAG and Welsh local authorities which have fortified their working relationships to deliver the waste strategy.

European Commission (2001) The Sixth Environment Action Programme *"Environment 2010: Our Future, Our Choice".*

National Assembly for Wales (2001) *Managing Wales Sustainably Consultation Paper,* July 2001.

National Assembly for Wales (2003) Municipal Waste Management Survey 2000/01, *Results of the Survey for Wales,* January 2003.

National Assembly for Wales (2004) http://www.businessenvironment.wales.gov.uk

National Statistics (2003), Economic Trends number 599, Norwich, HMSO.

VROM (2003) Netherlands Ministry of Spatial Planning, Housing and the Environment http://www.vrom.nl

Welsh Assembly Government (2001) *Planning Policy Wales, Technical Advice Note 21: Waste,* November 2001.

Welsh Assembly Government (2002a) *Guidance on Municipal Waste Management Strategies in Wales,* August 2002.

Welsh Assembly Government (2002b) *Wise About Waste: The National Waste Strategy for Wales,* June 2002

Welsh Development Agency (2002) *Update of the 1997 Review of the Welsh Environmental Goods and Services Sector*

Chapter 6

Building a Region's Sustainability Knowledge Base: Education for Sustainable Development in Wales

Ken Peattie

Introduction

The pursuit of sustainable development (SD) has become a widely accepted principle amongst governments, businesses and NGOs during the last twenty years. Although its importance is generally agreed upon, this can obscure the extent to which achieving greater sustainability requires a radical change to our perspectives, policies and practices. In framing its sustainability agenda in terms of *"Learning to Live Differently"* the Welsh Assembly Government (WAG) have very neatly summarised why making meaningful progress towards a more sustainable society and economy is a considerable challenge. It involves changing the way we live, which requires us to learn much that is new, and perhaps "unlearn" much that we currently accept without question.

Widespread acceptance of the importance of sustainable development amongst those in politics and business is vital if we are to make progress. It is not, however, sufficient in itself. Substantive progress will only be made if the wider population knows what sustainable development is, and understands why it is worth pursuing. Without this knowledge and understanding people will be unable to play their parts as consumers, voters, investors, managers, workers, parents and citizens. They will be left neither able to accept the changes that will be required, nor able to contribute effectively to making planned changes become a reality. Whether or not society can develop a strong sustainability knowledge base is therefore likely to be the determining factor in the success or failure of a whole raft of policies within the sustainable development agenda.

This makes *"How well do people understand the concept of 'sustainability'?"* a very important question. A 1995 study conducted by researchers from Lancaster University (MacNaughten et. al., 1995) revealed that:

"People generally are unfamiliar with the idea of 'sustainability' in its environmental sense. But once they understand it, they appear to identify positively with its values and priorities."

This finding was a surprise to many policymakers, coming eight years after the Brundtland Report (WCED, 1987) had apparently brought the concept of sustainability into the mainstream of political and social debate. Although this study could perhaps be dismissed as dated, and not particularly relevant to Wales, a 2002 survey by the Consumer Council of Wales (Bibbings, 2003) revealed that:

- 70% of Welsh consumers do not understand what sustainable development means;
- 5% believed that it related to construction;
- 18% believed it to be an economic term;

Those aged 35 to 54 were slightly more likely to understand what it means than younger or older consumers; even among the best-informed professionals and skilled white-collar workers (those in social classes ABC1), only 40 % were actually familiar with sustainable development.

These findings, which come five years after the Assembly Government accepted the statutory duty to promote sustainability enshrined in *The Government of Wales Act 1998*, demonstrate the problems involved in helping a region's population to become informed about, and engaged with, sustainability. The Welsh and UK Governments, and a whole range of local authorities, have put considerable efforts over the last five years into promoting sustainability and integrating its principles into many elements of their work. Developing genuine understanding about, and enthusiasm for, sustainability within the general population appears to be a much more difficult task than it appeared to be in the heady days of the Rio Summit on sustainable development in 1992.

This chapter explores some of the key issues involved in trying to strengthen the knowledge base relating to sustainability within Wales, particularly through education. The vast majority of these issues will also apply to other parts of the UK, and to other regions of Europe, irrespective of their educational and political systems.

Building a Sustainability Knowledge Base for Wales: The OSKaR Research Project

The research projects commissioned as part of the OSKaR initiative included one that focused on building the sustainability knowledge base of Wales, with the following aims:

- To better understand sources of sustainability knowledge and awareness within Wales by "mapping" the different sources, and exploring the relationships between them;
- To analyse Education for Sustainable Development (ESD) initiatives within formal education, with particular reference to:
  * the integration of available teaching resources into curriculum planning and teaching delivery;
  * progression in ESD, as learners move through formal education;
  * the relationship between sustainability within the curriculum and sustainability in the operations and management of schools;
  * the role of teacher training;
  * the relationship between Personal and Social Education (PSE) and other aspects of ESD;
- To explore the connections between the world of 'education' and the 'beyond-education' worlds of work and citizenship, in relation to sustainability issues;
- To investigate the extent to which sustainability knowledge and awareness is being developed through peoples' working lives, and particularly the extent to which campaigns aimed at engaging businesses in sustainability are reaching the workforce of companies;
- To identify best practice in promoting sustainability knowledge and awareness both within Wales and internationally.

This project was developed through an analysis of secondary sources; policy analysis using Welsh and UK policy documents; and a programme of interviews with key experts and stakeholders with an interest in sustainable development or education (and usually both). The interview programme included educators (sustainable development specialist and non-specialist teachers, and head teachers); members of Non-Governmental Organisations (NGOs) with an interest in ESD; educational support services (from both the statutory and voluntary sectors); local government officials responsible for education; Assembly Government officers responsible for sustainable development; and a range of other relevant stakeholders. Space constraints make listing them all impossible, but it is appropriate to thank them all for their valuable contribution. This is particularly the case for the ESD Advisory Panel that supports the Assembly Government, who were extremely generous with their time, and in sharing their own research, expertise and experiences.

The project covered more issues than can be encapsulated within a single book chapter. The focus of this chapter is therefore on a sub-set of the challenges and complications confronting those seeking to develop the sustainability knowledge base of Wales and on some of the innovative practices encountered within Wales. It also seeks to highlight those areas where changes to public policy may present opportunities to contribute to building knowledge and awareness about sustainability in the future.

Reviewing Education for Sustainable Development

"Education for sustainable development is about the learning needed to maintain and improve our quality of life and the quality of life of generations to come. It is about equipping individuals, communities, groups, businesses and government to live and act sustainably; as well as giving them an understanding of the environmental, social and economic issues involved. It is about preparing for the world in which we will live in the next century, and making sure that we are not found wanting". (DETR, 1999)

This project is part of a recent growth trend in research into ESD in Wales and other parts of the UK. In November 2002 the booklet *Education for Sustainable Development and Global Citizenship* (ACCAC, 2002) was published to explain and promote ESD to Welsh schools and provide examples of good practice from which they could learn. It outlined the key concepts of ESD and global citizenship as being :

- **interdependence**: understanding how people, the environment and the economy are inextricably linked at all levels from local to global;
- **citizenship and stewardship**: recognising the importance of taking individual responsibility and action to make the world a better place;
- **needs and rights**: understanding our own basic needs and about human rights and the implications for the needs of future generations of actions taken today;
- **diversity**: understanding, respecting and valuing both human diversity – cultural, social and economic – and biodiversity;
- **sustainable change**: understanding that resources are finite and that this has implications for people's lifestyles and for commerce and industry;

- **quality of life**: acknowledging that global equity and justice are essential elements of sustainability and that basic needs must be met universally;
- **uncertainty and precaution**: acknowledging that there are a range of possible approaches to sustainability and global citizenship and that situations are constantly changing, indicating a need for flexibility and lifelong learning;
- **values and perceptions**: developing a critical evaluation of images of, and information about, the less and more economically developed parts of the world and an appreciation of the effect these have on people's attitudes and values;
- **conflict resolution**: understanding how conflicts are a barrier to development and a risk to us all and why there is a need for their resolution and the promotion of harmony.

During 2002 there was also a review of the *Personal and Social Education (PSE) Framework* commissioned by the Qualifications, Curriculum and Assessment Authority for Wales (ACCAC). This revealed that although many in education found the framework helpful in delivering the Assembly Government's three underlying themes, it was typically more helpful in dealing with equal opportunities and social inclusion, than sustainability.

England's School Inspectorate, the Office for Standard's in Education (Ofsted), in 2003 produced *Taking the First Step Forward: Towards an Education for sustainable development*, a guide to good practice in primary and secondary schools. This was based around a study of 26 schools and concluded that although individual schools tended to be unique in their approach to ESD, there were common characteristics of excellence that included:

- a record of thinking about such issues over a number of years;
- a whole-school commitment to integrate ESD into the work of the school and a well-developed local support network;
- strong links with the community, in particular to encourage pupils and their families to play a part in their local community;
- pupils who demonstrate both individual and collective responsibility in looking after and improving their learning environment and an emphasis on promoting positive attitudes and values to aid their learning now and in the future;
- a well planned curriculum, taught by teachers who have clear objectives and an active involvement of pupils in initiatives that promote ESD.

February 2003 saw the publication of *Learning To Last: The Government's Sustainable Development Education Strategy For England* from the Sustainable Development

Education Panel for England (SDEP, 2003). This highlighted the need for a coherent strategy on ESD and stressed that:

"The challenge is to win hearts and minds and to motivate people to take personal action. This will not happen without mobilising channels of informal communication, including the media, youth and trade associations, non-governmental organisations of all kinds, museums, libraries, galleries, the arts, sports and many more. What is needed is a positive vision reinforced by a simple, consistent message expressed in plain language."

In Wales, March 2003 saw the spotlight move beyond schooling with *"ESD: The Challenge for Higher, Further and Adult Education"* a conference and workshops held at University of Wales, Swansea. This concluded strongly that within the tertiary education sector, there is much that needs to be done to improve engagement with ESD, and set out comprehensive short, medium and long-term recommendations on how to improve this situation.

In terms of Initial Teacher Education and Training (ITET), during 2002/2003 the Welsh Assembly's ESD Advisory Panel and Working Group on Global Citizenship combined to review how those involved in ITET could better embed ESD and Citizenship issues into teacher training. The review was followed by an ITET related conference in May 2003. Within its findings the review highlighted :

- The need to facilitate a constructive partnership between schools, colleges and educational support providers;
- The need to develop better ways to share good practice and materials between the eight Welsh ITET colleges;
- The need to provide support materials for both students and staff;
- The need for stronger official guidance and statutory policy support to ensure that ESD and Global Citizenship are embedded within all aspects of ITET Colleges including their constitutions, objectives, management systems and inspections.

In July 2003, the UK Parliament's Environmental Audit Committee published *Learning the Sustainability Lesson* (EAC, 2003) which reviewed all elements of education policy and sought to develop a more integrated vision of the future development of education and training strategy and the strategy for sustainable development.

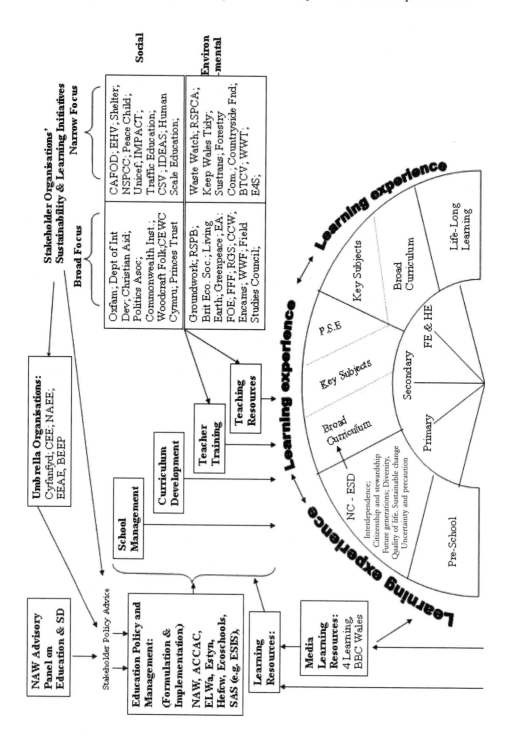

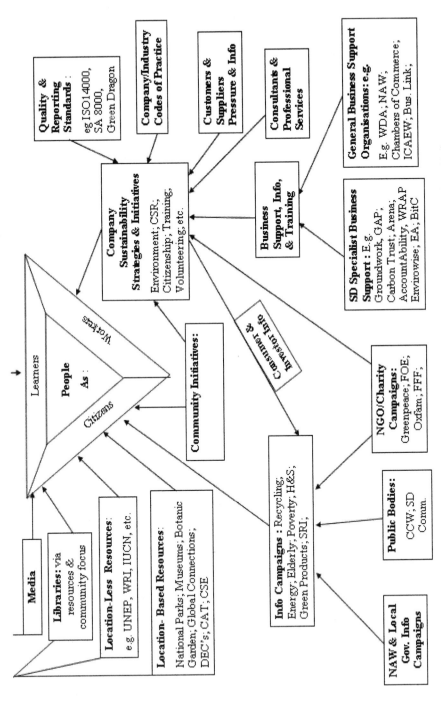

Figure 6.1. Mapping Sources of Sustainability Knowledge and awareness in Wales

Mapping sources of knowledge and awareness about Sustainable Development

When awareness about sustainable development is discussed, the context is usually formal education and the school curriculum in particular. However, there are many settings and stages in a person's life in which they can learn more about sustainability issues. One of this project's aims was to "map" the key sources of knowledge and awareness about SD in Wales. A simplified version of the results of this mapping exercise is presented in Figure 6.1.

Although this diagram contains more arrows and boxes than a national archery contest, it is not intended to bewilder, but instead to demonstrate the complexity of the issues involved in building an effective sustainability knowledge base for a region.

The map envisages three "roles" in which people can gain knowledge and awareness about sustainable development:

1. **As learners**: within the formal learning process, including schools, tertiary education and also through life-long learning (Pre-school learning is including within this role for simplicity, and to reflect growing interest in sustainable development in "Early Years" provision);
2. **As workers**: since sustainability may feature in peoples' working lives through training, or if issues of environmental sustainability, corporate social responsibility or community involvement form part of their employer's strategic agenda or policies;
3. **As citizens**: since sustainability knowledge and awareness can develop within individuals' private lives from media coverage, political debate, or through the efforts of firms or community or campaigning groups.

Although drawing such distinctions can be helpful for the purpose of analysis and discussion, they should not be interpreted too rigidly. The workplace is an important source of learning for many, and citizens who are also parents are quite likely to learn from educational materials aimed at their children.

For the purposes of this chapter, the bulk of the discussion is focused on ESD and formal learning. This reflects its crucial role in promoting the future understanding and awareness of sustainability within regions such as Wales. It should also be remembered however, that it alone is not the answer to developing a sustainability knowledge base. However good it is, in the short-term, ESD within our schools and colleges will only reach one generation at a time. As the *Learning the Sustainability Lesson* report stressed, success will depend on using all the available channels (EAC, 2003).

Reaching citizens

Before focusing on ESD for learners, it is worth briefly outlining the other components of the map, including those relating to how citizens and workers learn about sustainability. Reaching citizens with sustainability information can be achieved in a number of ways including:

- **The media**: Wildlife programmes; news coverage of environmental disasters, poverty or development issues; and local media coverage featuring problems or progress in promoting sustainability within individual communities, can all play an important part in awareness raising. The willingness and ability of policy-makers to harness the media to communicate about sustainability varies between countries and regions. An interesting example comes from Mexico, where their local franchise for the *"Big Brother"* TV show (watched by 80 % of young people with access to a TV) has been encouraged by the government to adopt conservation of water and energy, and recycling as components of the programme. Therefore as well as competing to complete ludicrous tasks or achieve social popularity, the contestants are also judged weekly by the audience in terms of their performance as environmentalists. Such enthusiasm isn't currently exhibited in the Welsh media. As Bibbings (2003) highlights within Wales "The media believe the term (SD) to be a turn-off for readers, as do businesses and advertisers, and so consumers do not come across it often enough for it to sink in."
- **Libraries**: Library resources are an important source of information about other countries and cultures, and environmental issues. This information can benefit learners seeking to study, but also help to inform citizens following up on their interests, hobbies or travel plans.
- **Internet resources**: The world-wide web contains everything anyone could possibly want to know in relation to sustainability, the environment and a range of social causes and community issues. The Internet provides some particular advantages in terms of developing knowledge and understanding about sustainable development. It allows the sharing of common interests and knowledge, and it can deliver this on a global or local basis with equal ease.
- **Location-based resources**: Many people develop a greater understanding of sustainability issues through visiting particular locations. Within Wales, National Parks and nature reserves have well-developed educational resources and programmes, which can both support school trips and education, and inform a wider audience.

- **Public information campaigns**: These are a very traditional means by which policy makers inform the general public on issues such as recycling, road safety, and energy conservation.
- **Political campaigning**: Given the centrality of "quality of life" to the sustainability debate, it is not surprising that many sustainability issues are central to political campaigning, even if they are not explicitly framed in terms of sustainable development.
- **Public bodies**: for example the Countryside Council for Wales, whose responsibilities include providing information and publicity to help protect and promote places of interest and natural beauty within Wales;
- **NGOs**: Although many NGOs have specific educational support initiatives for schools, their campaigning work can also raise awareness of issues for the general public.
- **Community initiatives**: People may become more aware about sustainability through interest or involvement in local social or environmental projects and community regeneration. The work of community–orientated organisations such as Groundwork plays a vital role in this.
- **Company communications for customers or investors**: There are fewer explicit environmental marketing claims aimed at consumers today than was the case in the mid 1990s. However in certain markets such as food, concern about issues of animal welfare, pesticide residues and the growing demand for organic and fairly-traded produce have encouraged many companies to develop and communicate responses to these issues. There is also a growing market in socially responsible investment, and social, ethical and environmental disclosure to investors is now provided by 73 % of the UK's top 250 companies.

Reaching workers

There are a number of ways in which people can learn about sustainability through their working lives. In a region like Wales, where there is a statutory duty to pursue and promote sustainability, and a high proportion of employment provided by the public sector, there is a major opportunity to use the workplace as a communication channel. In the private sector, people are most likely to engage with sustainability issues when it is part of the strategy of their employers. Interaction with suppliers, customers or trade associations may all act as sources of information and motivators for firms in addressing sustainability.

For companies who seek to develop strategies for environmental management or community engagement, there are a range of organisations who will provide help and information. Some of these, such as Groundwork and Arena Network focus primarily on sustainability issues. Others such as the Welsh Development Agency or the Federation of Small Businesses provide sustainability information as part of a much broader business support agenda. Business information initiatives vary in the extent to which they succeed in informing the actual workforce of the company, rather than just its management and strategy.

Reaching learners

The model identifies four key components of education, which influence peoples' learning ESD experience:

1. Curriculum development and delivery; particularly in terms of the national curriculum for ESD;
2. Teacher training: in-service and through teacher training colleges;
3. Teaching resources: including materials provided through the education system and those from external organisations;
4. The management of schools: since this can play an important part in reinforcing classroom content on ESD;

These four elements are all in turn strongly influenced by education policy from government and its implementation through agencies such as Local Education Authorities (LEAs). There are a number of stakeholder organisations involved in the development and implementation of education policy including:

- **Funding bodies** such as ELWa and the Higher Education Funding Council of Wales;
- **Inspection service providers**. Several organisations provide school inspections, which can be a powerful lever for implementing change in education. The principle inspector is Estyn, HM's Inspectorate for Education and Training in Wales. In 2002 Estyn published guidelines for inspecting and evaluating ESD;
- **Support services for schools**. This includes statutory support, such as from Estyn and ACCAC for the curriculum, and voluntary sector support, such as from Eco-Schools for environmental management in schools.
- **Campaigning Groups and other NGOs**. A range of NGOs are also actively involved in supporting schools in delivering ESD.

All of these also provide advice and support to policy makers, and many are also represented in the principle mechanism for policy support for the National Assembly, its Advisory Panel on ESD.

External teaching resource providers

The teaching resources made available to schools and colleges form an important influence on ESD delivery. The number of providers, and the variety of resources, has recently grown significantly. The map divides them into four, somewhat arbitrary, categories on two dimensions:

1. **Primarily Social or Environmental.** Relatively few organisations seek to contribute learning resources for sustainability, which encompass the entire agenda, or even focus on the third, economic dimension. Most are either primarily social or environmental in their focus. Having said that, many people argue for a move away from such delineation, and some organisations that once had a clear humanitarian/social focus are becoming increasingly interested in also addressing environmentally related causes of human/social problems (as is the case with Oxfam);
2. **Broad or Narrow Focus.** Some organisations focus on a broad swathe of the sustainability agenda while others focus on a single issue. The RSPB might sound like a single issue organisation, but its interests go far beyond birds themselves, to encompass a range of issues relating to biodiversity, habitat protection and environmental quality. By contrast, Shelter focuses tightly on their key issue of homelessness. In reality providers represent a continuum, rather than a dichotomy, but a rough sorting into broad or narrow categories is possible and potentially helpful.

These are not the only important differences between information providers. They can also be classified in terms of whether their focus is Welsh, UK or beyond; and whether the provision of teaching materials is their primary role or secondary to it. It can also be helpful to distinguish between campaigning groups and educational initiatives. Some initiatives are definitely campaigns that aim to create movement towards a particular goal beyond education, whilst others are aimed at education as their primary goal. Drawing definite boundaries between them can be difficult.

Location-less Resources

Teachers and learners increasingly have opportunities to take advantage of sustainability-related information resources around the globe via the Internet. Examples include:

* The Department of International Development's *Global Dimension* web site which provides a range of materials to support PSE (www.globaldimension.org.uk);

- Site of the *'Environment and Schools Initiatives'* Project in the OECD region-includes projects and initiatives by country (www.ensi.org);
- *'State of Global Environment'* which includes a directory of environmental education training opportunities (www.unep.org);
- World Resources Institute *'Centre for Education'* site (www.wri.org/enved/);

Location-based Resources:

Knowledge and awareness about sustainable development can also be reinforced for learners at particular locations offering more practical sustainable development learning opportunities. Examples within Wales include:

- Centre for Alternative Technology at Machynlleth, widely regarded as Europe's leading Eco-Centre;
- Global Connections (a World Studies Resource Centre, in Pembroke);
- Development Education Centres (DECs);
- Association of National Park Authorities (ANPA);
- National Botanic Garden of Wales & Botanic Gardens Education Network;
- West Wales Eco-Centre;
- Environment Centre, Swansea.

Key issues from the Map

ESD stakeholders mostly found the map useful, partly because it served to highlight the complexities involved in developing a sustainability knowledge base. It also proved a useful framework around which to structure discussions about the role of individual stakeholders in contributing to ESD, and their perceptions of the key issues involved in developing the sustainability knowledge base of Wales. The following points reflect some of the key issues to emerge from those discussions:

Progression in education

One theme, which emerged from the project interviews, was the way in which the approach to sustainability changes as children progress through the educational system. In primary schools the approach to sustainability is often very broad and cross-curricular. This is reflected in projects that span across a number of subject areas. In secondary education there is a greater tendency for consideration of sustainability to be concentrated in particular parts of the curriculum. So for example, environmental issues may be viewed as belonging to geography, biodiversity issues could be tackled in biology, and many social issues would tend to be seen as a part of PSE. There can also be a tendency for broader coverage of sustainability issues to be concentrated in particular school years, for example "Year 9" before GCSE work commences. In tertiary education, this tendency for sustainability issues to be captured within particular elements of the curriculum goes even further. Despite the findings and good intentions of the *Toyne Report* (DFE, 1993), which stressed the importance of integrating sustainability into all subject areas, most students can escape exposure to it unless they choose a subject such as environmental science, or an option such as development economics. So ironically as a person progresses through the education system towards citizenship and employment, the consideration of sustainability issues tends to dissipate rather than intensify.

The primary/secondary education watershed

One important aspect of the progression through the educational system, in terms of the promotion of ESD, is the watershed represented by the transition between primary and secondary education. Primary schools appear to find it far easier to integrate sustainability considerations across the curriculum and throughout the life and management of the school. This is reflected in the much higher uptake of sustainability related schemes such as Eco-Schools, where primary schools outnumber secondary schools in Wales at a ratio of 5 to 1. Similarly in reviews of good practice from both Wales and the rest of the UK, there seem to be more examples to choose from amongst primary schools.

A number of reasons were suggested for this. It may be a reflection of the difference in size between the two, with a secondary school being a much larger and more complex organisation within which to apply sustainability principles within. Primary schools also tend to have a greater emphasis on values, cross-curricular projects, closeness to the community and what was described by many as a *"family atmosphere"*, all of which were seen as being helpful in addressing ESD. In secondary schools a number of characteristics were seen as working against the integration of ESD including :

- the emphasis on testing and qualifications;
- the emphasis on the curriculum and the boundaries between subjects, and the tendency to have teachers who are subject specialists and used to thinking within disciplines rather than across them;
- interests among the older age group of children which tend to work against greater engagement with sustainability (not least of which is an emerging interest in the opposite sex !).

Within South Wales' Education Support and Inspection Service (ESIS), an innovative project to promote ESD is currently underway which follows "action research" principles in helping schools to design and implement ESD strategies. One interesting aspect of this project, was the bringing together of head teachers from the primary and secondary schools involved, to learn from each other about good practice in ESD. The secondary heads, for example, were able to benefit from the primary heads' experience in running cross-curricular ESD projects.

Box 6.1. Innovation in Wales : Cardiff Waste Forum's Schools Composting Project.

This innovative approach to ESD represents "joined up" policy-making at its best. Schools are encouraged to begin composting with the provision of a compost bin, teachers' toolkit, and tools (provided by B&Q to demonstrate a community/business link). Children are encouraged to eat only fruit as break-time snacks, and to compost the waste. Fruit is provided within schools, and often used as part of a reward system. In addition to learning about the value of composting (and its use in enriching the school grounds), the project also effectively encourages healthy diets and reduces school litter.

The supporting teaching materials help teachers to use the compost project across a range of curriculum subjects including practical maths, science, IT and geography.

The tertiary education conundrum

The importance of delivering sustainable development knowledge and awareness within post-school education is widely acknowledged, particularly in relation to Universities:

> "*Universities educate most of the people who develop and manage society's institutions. For this reason, universities bear profound responsibilities to increase the awareness, knowledge, technologies, and tools to create an environmentally sustainable future*". (Tailloires Declaration, UPFS 1995).

This logic was embodied in the 1993 Toyne Report into integrating the environment into the curriculum, which sought to promote sustainability within the management of universities and its integration into the curriculum for every discipline. Unfortunately this philosophical strength may also have been a practical weakness. In practice it allowed those responsible for the disciplines offering the most scope for progress to downplay its relevance through criticism of the worth and feasibility of integrating sustainability into the curriculum for English, Art and Language departments. The *Review of the Toyne Report* (SCAA, 1996) commented on *"considerable indifference"* within higher education and found that *"Hardly any progress has been made in respect of curriculum 'greening'"*.

There are certain disciplines, where integration of sustainability principles into the curriculum across Wales and the UK could make a significant contribution to developing a more sustainable society. If departments teaching business and management, economics, accountancy and social policy can create a generation of managers, economists, professional investors, accountants and policy makers who understand the principles of sustainability, hope will increase for all of us. Sadly, in practice, University Departments such as Business Schools have often been among the most reluctant to integrate sustainability into their teaching (Coopey, 2001). There are however some examples of good practice within Wales. Within Cardiff Business School, sustainability themes recur in a number of undergraduate and post-graduate courses (often in the context of corporate social responsibility). For the Business Administration degree, one quarter of the compulsory final year undergraduate core course in *Strategic Management* is dedicated to sustainability principles and their impact on business strategy and practice. Cardiff's School of City and Regional Planning provides one of the few UK masters level courses to focus on sustainability including business issues, and the University of Wales, Bangor has pioneered an undergraduate degree in sustainable development. In terms of integrating sustainability throughout both the curriculum and the fabric of tertiary education institutions, Wales also has one of the leading academic thinkers in Rolf Jucker of University of Wales, Swansea (see Jucker, 2002).

A controversial role for testing

Progress testing is central to education in the UK and beyond. It also provokes controversy about the quantity, nature and timing of assessments, in relation to ESD. The perceived reality within many schools is that students and staff have learnt to focus their energies on things that are assessed. Those who support testing for elements of ESD, see it as a vital way to signal its importance to both students and staff. This thinking lies behind the Welsh Joint Education Council's plans to develop a GCSE short-course in PSE.

Critics of testing and qualifications related to ESD understand the message that the introduction of testing and qualifications sends, and the benefits that this might bring, but point out the difficulties and negative consequences that might also arise. An emphasis on testing is often viewed as tending to reinforce an *"education about sustainable development"* approach, centring on knowledge and the testing of that knowledge. It is much more difficult to assess *"education for sustainable development"* in terms of students learning critical thinking skills, communications abilities, and development of their personal values and sense of empathy and responsibility. Many of these aspects of ESD will only truly be tested outside of school, in terms of how students live their lives. Therefore critics highlight the problems of devising meaningful tests. Another concern about testing that was raised, relates to subjects like global citizenship, where stakeholders were concerned that a student who performed poorly in an assessment would assume that this made them a *"bad citizen"*.

The importance of teacher training

In any region, new educational developments such as the integration of ESD will first require education and training for teachers. For new teachers this comes through initial teacher education and training (ITET), which in the UK is delivered either through a three-year B.Ed. degree, or a one-year Postgraduate Certificate of Education (PGCE). Training of new teachers in ESD will ultimately improve the capacity of schools to embrace and promote ESD in the long-term. In the short-term, it is also important to reach existing staff through in-service training, which in the UK is delivered via "inset days".

In Wales, an ESD Advisory Panel project recently reviewed the Welsh Teacher Training Colleges. They found that colleges varied in the degree to which they had attempted to integrate sustainability into their own ITET curriculum, and that there had been relatively little progress in integrating sustainability principles into teacher training beyond trying to impart knowledge about it to teachers. Most colleges were reliant on external specialists acting as "guest speakers" to cover key elements of sustainability. The challenge is to spread good practices evolving at Trinity College and University of Wales, Bangor throughout Wales.

As with the curriculum for schools themselves, the problem in teacher training is that promoting sustainable development can be perceived as just one of several new demands that need to be accommodated into an already packed course. This is particularly acute with PGCE courses. Due to the emphasis on training within schools, the teaching time in which teachers are themselves learning away from the schools, can amount to only 12 weeks out of a 32-week course. One suggested solution to this problem is to develop on-line and interactive self-study materials on sustainability to educate trainee teachers. One such resource has been produced by Unesco. Developing new resources, tailored to the educational needs of particular regions, may also prove helpful.

In terms of the use of inset training for ESD, in-service training time is another precious commodity that other issues also compete for. In some areas, "twilight" after school training sessions for ESD had been tried. Attendance at these had often been disappointing, partly because the hours posed problems for teachers who themselves had children, and partly because no incentives were provided for teachers to attend.

Putting aside additional time for staff training is one possible solution to this. Another is that when teachers undertake sustainability related in-service training, it contributes to their future salary scale progress. Although this might tend to attract criticism as potentially expensive, it is sobering to consider that such a system is already in place in Mexico, which is a comparatively poor country. Another possibility is to put ESD on an equal footing with issues like health and safety training, which are simply inescapable, and for which training time must be allocated.

Box 6.2. Innovation in Wales : Embedding Education for Global Citizenship and Sustainable Development in ITET Courses.

The World Education Centre for North Wales based in Bangor, is working with the School of Education in the University of Wales, Bangor on a three year project which aims to embed education for global citizenship and sustainable development in initial teacher education and training courses. Initial project work has involved identifying and supporting ESD practices within current college courses and School Experience; developing information packs for students; and disseminating examples of good practice and other materials. The ultimate aim is to provide a model of effective integration of ESD into ITET that can be applied throughout Wales.

Official guidance and statutory policy support

Although there is widespread support for the aims and values of ESD development within the educational system, often it is statutory requirements that were viewed as a key to instigating change. One key driver in terms of setting priorities and determining progress is the use of performance indicators and the schools' inspection service. The inclusion of sustainability within the new common inspection framework from Estyn was widely perceived as a crucial step forward in promoting ESD. One driver that has not yet been utilised in Wales is to make it compulsory to include ESD within LEAs' strategic plans. Doing so would ensure that schools then included it within their own development plans.

As well as making ESD a mandatory part of teacher training, it could be made a part of training for school governors, with a mandatory requirement for a governor to be responsible for overseeing ESD provision in each school. There was a perception that governors are generally very receptive to ESD principles, but training time available for governors is typically very constrained, and there tended to be a preoccupation with those areas that represent statutory responsibilities.

Integrating sustainable development into schools management

It is increasingly widely recognised that delivering ESD in practice cannot simply be achieved by including knowledge about sustainable development issues within the curriculum. If students are taught about the importance of sustainable development principles in a classroom, but then witness these principles being ignored or contradicted in the way the rest of the school operates, the lesson about sustainability is unlikely to be heeded or learnt. Embracing ESD poses a challenge to integrate its principles into all aspects of school management and life. The case for taking a sustainability approach to schools management has an environmental and economic dimension as well. A study of the sustainability of Britain's schools system (SEC/ME 2001) revealed that the education of Britain's schoolchildren accounts for around 5 % of total government expenditure and generates an energy bill of over £ 100 million per annum. Educational buildings alone are also responsible for more than 5 % of CO_2 emissions from non-domestic buildings in the UK.

Across Europe an important pathway for schools to operate in a more sustainable way is the Eco-Schools programme. This programme has its roots in the Local Agenda 21 response to the Rio sustainability summit in 1992, and was originally relatively narrowly focused on environmental science and environmental management. The Eco-Schools Programme encourages a pupil-led response to environmental and sustainability issues. It provides a structured system for schools based on ISO 14001 environmental management system principles. In recent years the programme has broadened in Wales to consider issues relating to health and development, but the key issues are typically litter and waste minimisation, energy and water conservation, and school grounds development.

An important element of Eco-Schools is the use of an Eco-Committee including pupils, staff, governors and parents which review progress, develop plans and encourage involvement. In other schools, a school council can play a similar role in encouraging pupils, staff and other stakeholders to discuss sustainability issues and the school's response to them. There were examples of school councils taking a lead in initiatives such as providing healthier and fairly-traded snack foods within schools. The move towards making school councils compulsory should provide many schools with a fresh opportunity to address ESD issues both in the curriculum and the practical workings of the school.

In terms of promoting ESD within schools, examples of good practice throughout Wales and beyond tend to share one defining characteristic: someone who champions ESD within the school. This may be the head teacher, a teacher from an ESD-related area such as Geography, or simply a teacher or governor with a real enthusiasm for the issue. In secondary schools in particular, the active support of head teachers was seen as crucial for Eco-Schools membership or other forms of ESD initiatives to succeed.

Box 6.3. Innovation in Wales : Environmental Management Systems for Schools.

In addition to an Eco-Schools programme which includes over 500 schools, Wales has developed its own unique programmes to integrate ESD principles beyond the curriculum and into all aspects of a school. One example is the Sustainability Application Framework in Education (SAFE) project led by Carmarthenshire Council. This seeks to take the sustainable development principles that they were already promoting through the Eco-Schools programme, to create a more holistic approach to sustainable development in teaching, school management and staff development. The approach taken by SAFE has been to combine environmental management principles derived from the "Natural Step" methodology and to work with partners including Forum for the Future and Eco-Schools to make all aspects of a school more sustainable. In Pembrokeshire, a similar "Sustainable Schools" awards project has sought to integrate Eco-Schools initiatives with elements of the "Healthy Schools" and development education initiative to create a holistic system.

Turning information into knowledge

One apparently promising development in the quest to integrate sustainability concepts into formal education is the growth in the resources and information available to support teachers. However, talking to ESD stakeholders, it is clear that the current approach to the creation of educational materials is characterised by a great deal of duplication, insufficient matching of resources to educational needs, and often a failure to connect the resources provided with the teachers who need them. Many different examples were provided. Head teachers could point to large volumes of materials that would accumulate in their offices, and which they did not have the time to assess, to judge their quality, appropriate level, and relevant place in the curriculum. Teachers provided examples of ESD software sent to them, which could not be reliably uploaded onto school computer networks and so went unused. An NGO related a tale of how it accessed a database of teachers to target their educational pack into the hands of the appropriate teachers, only to have many of them returned because the teachers in question had moved on, or the address for the school was incorrect. Other examples related to UK focused organisations, who failed to recognise the differences in the educational systems in Wales, Scotland and England. This led to materials being sent out in regions to support courses.

There were other problems related to the provision of teaching materials. There were genuine concerns among stakeholders about the role that educational materials can play in promoting particular agendas. It is widely recognised that whether an organisation is a business, a trade body, an arm of government or a campaigning group, in developing an educational resource, it will do so to meet its own objectives. The partiality of many resources can be used to educational advantage. Very aware teachers were perfectly able to juxtapose materials representing opposing camps (for example an oil company and a campaigning organisation like Greenpeace) for discussion by students. Less aware or less experienced teachers may tend to use only a single source to cover a particular issue. A problem for schools that were struggling to get to grips with the ESD agenda was that their response could become driven by the availability of materials. A professionally-produced set of resources could be seized upon as "the answer" to teaching sustainability issues, regardless of its breadth and the agenda that lay behind its production. Another issue was the degree to which educational materials from organisations were actually planned around the learning needs of students and the teaching, rather than around the communication or campaigning needs of the information provider. Although materials would typically come with a curriculum map, this was often judged to be inadequate and not sufficiently backed up by the type of detailed lesson plans and other insights provided by the best materials.

There are several different approaches that can be adopted when attempting to deal with the danger of "information overload" which faces teachers seeking to access material to develop and support ESD:

- **Do nothing**. One argument is that the best resources to support ESD will emerge if diversity and initiative are encouraged, and that it would be a mistake to try to manage this process for the sake of efficiency.
- **Signpost**. A first step in trying to help teachers to deal with the wealth of resources is to develop information resources to guide them towards what is available. An innovative Welsh project that tackled this issue is a *Virtual Directory*, commissioned by the Assembly Government's ESD panel and produced in association with Oxfam and the RSPB.
- **Kitemark**. One approach to helping teachers to find the best and most relevant materials to support ESD would be to have some form of quality standard or "kitemark". This is a controversial idea, which poses many questions about who should provide the quality assurance and what criteria will be used.
- **Combine**. An approach that can combine some of the benefits of "kitemarking" while still encouraging diversity and initiative is to combine particular resources into "themed" packs. Examples of this particular approach have been emerging within Wales. Keep Wales Tidy have collated a pack of materials relating to waste.

Oxfam have produced a catalogue *Resources for Schools* which combines their own materials with others from Christian Aid, Amnesty International and the Development Education Centres. Such packs are very popular with schools.

- **Become interactive**. Another approach to providing guidance for teachers on the value and use of particular resources is to collate the feedback from teachers themselves. A further planned development of the *Virtual Directory* will allow teachers to post feedback on resources, much as purchasers using e-commerce sites such as Amazon can.

- **Co-ordinate**. The production of ESD educational resources is often driven as much by the funding requirements linked to many sustainability projects, as to a desire on the part of organisations to communicate and educate. One opportunity to reduce the duplication within ESD resources might be to develop a strategic framework of resource needs to support ESD teaching. This could be broken down across all age groups and across relevant elements of the curriculum and other aspects of school life, perhaps linked to the evolving National Grid for Learning project. Organisations bidding for public funds for sustainability projects that are looking to develop related educational resources could then be steered by funders towards under-supported elements of ESD.

The importance of human support

Educators are faced with a greater array of ESD policy advice and guidance, and related on-line and on-paper teaching resources, than ever before. Ultimately however, teachers depend on some form of human face-to-face support to help them to navigate and use these resources. Support services were often crucial in instigating ESD developments in schools, and guiding teachers in terms of the issues and resources. Such support can come from a number of sources. In the case of Wales, LEAs will provide specialist support staff either individually, or by combining together to create joint support services such as ESIS (which covers Merthyr Tydfil, Bridgend, Caerphilly and Rhondda Cynon Taff) and Cynnal (covering Gwynedd and Anglesey). Support is also offered by organisations such as ACCAC, Estyn and CCW. Support is also often provided by many NGOs and other organisations in relation to the educational materials that they produce.

There are a number of issues linked to the provision of ESD support. For many LEAs their support team will have to cover a wide range of elements of education, which will not allow for an ESD specialist. It is more typical to find it being included as a sub-set of the responsibilities of a subject specialist in an area such as geography. There are also trends that are tending to reduce the level of educational support being provided by organisations. One is a move away from central educational support posts in a number of NGOs and public bodies. Often these organisations see this as a positive move in which responsibility for educational support is shared, and pushed out more to the "front line" of their operation. In practice however the effect is usually to decrease the overall hours devoted to educational support. Another common approach is to focus instead on those who train teachers, or those who work in educational support within the LEAs. Although potentially efficient, it does depend on there being sufficient room in the teacher training curriculum, and staff time available within the support services, to deliver support to individual schools.

ESD beyond the classroom

Stakeholders in ESD are unanimous in emphasising the importance of getting children out of the classroom to learn about the environment, their community and the way that people live in other places. However, despite general agreement that ESD greatly benefits from outdoor learning and trips, there are a number of obstacles emerging in the UK that deter schools from planning trips. Pressure on financial resources is one barrier for most schools. In poorer communities, whose children may be those offered the least opportunity to travel other than through the school, even heavily subsidised trips can suffer large portions of a year group withdrawing because parents cannot afford to make the requested contribution. Concerns about safety on school trips in the wake of a small number of high profile accidents, mounting insurance costs and concerns about teachers' potential liabilities amongst teaching unions are all also acting as disincentives. Rising insurance costs for outdoor pursuits centres are also threatening their businesses which may further reduce the opportunities for outdoor learning in Wales.

Finally, sheer timetable pressure can make it difficult to find the necessary time to transport children any significant distance for educational visits. Faced with delivering the national curriculum and pressure to achieve examination-based performance targets, head teachers may want to increase the number of external trips their children make, but often feel obliged to reduce them instead. This may mean making a choice between cultural trips to the theatre, visits to historical sites or visits to environmentally orientated resources.

Education outside the classroom does not necessarily have to involve travel. Many schools are looking to use their own grounds for the purposes of environmental education, particularly through involvements with organisations such as *Learning through Landscapes*. Using the school grounds as an education resource effectively does require ESD to be integrated into the management of the school and its grounds as well. Stories emerged of examples where the two had clearly failed to connect. One school had established a wildflower meadow that has been carefully nurtured by pupils and was being used as a resource to teach about biology and biodiversity. Unfortunately it was lost during the school holidays when contractors responsible for the management of school grounds treated it with weedkiller.

Balancing the global and local dimensions of sustainable development

One of the strengths of ESD, as it has been promoted within the UK, is that it has sought to put sustainability in its proper global context. This is particularly true in Wales, through the integration of ESD and Global Citizenship education. However, amongst those delivering and supporting ESD in practice, there were concerns expressed that perhaps the emphasis on the global dimensions of sustainability had acted to overshadow its local dimensions.

In areas of research relating to sustainability, such as attempts to encourage more responsible consumer behaviour, the issue of *"perceived personal relevance"* has been shown to be one of the only consistent and significant influences on peoples' behaviour. Although people can be made to feel concerned about the sustainability of the environment, the community and the state of society, they are only likely to change their behaviour when they perceive these issues in terms of our environment, our community and our society. This is not to argue that schools should not teach about global environmental problems, and the global problems of poverty and development. They should, but they should ensure that there is also the right balance in terms of connecting to these issues at a local level. Even in global development education, the use of the Internet to connect schools in Wales with other classes in developing countries through discussion groups can allow these issues to be addressed in terms of *"my e-penpal"*.

The problem in terms of making connections to the local dimensions of ESD is that good resources to support such teaching may not exist. Some teachers highlighted the irony that it was relatively easy to engage students in concerns about the threat to the Amazonian rainforest, yet often there were local forestry resources under threat, that were never visited or studied by local schools. Similarly teachers were aware of the benefits of visiting key national and regional ESD resources such as the National Botanic Garden of Wales, the National Museum of Welsh Life at St. Fagans or one of Wales' Development Education Centres. However, they were often deterred from doing so because of the problems relating to school trips outlined above, and because often it was simply not feasible for a school to accommodate an entire year group (which for a Secondary School could number over 200) at a single location. Even for day trips, many of the locations that could provide significant educational benefits, also lacked the necessary interpretation facilities (such as lecture theatres) which could cater for such large numbers.

For teachers there was a clear demand for high quality teaching materials to support

ESD that related to places and resources in their school's locality. This could be achieved in a number of ways. Local libraries could collate and house relevant materials, which could then be accessed by all local schools. This could be particularly useful for primary schools whose relatively small year sizes could allow such resource to be accessed in turn. There are a number of ways that such resources could be assembled, beyond simply collating existing information within libraries with the aim of developing it into an ESD resource, including :

- developing through links with local historical societies;
- taking advantage of community-based information technology initiatives such as virtual community scrap-books or verbal histories from local residents;
- forging connections between any local tourism resources relating to eco-tourism, industrial archaeology or social history;

Linking to the world beyond school

A very important dimension of the ESD provided in schools is the extent to which it helps to inform and shape peoples' lives once they leave school. Perhaps the greatest danger facing ESD is that what people learn in relation to sustainability is regarded like history or algebra; important perhaps, but not relevant to the everyday lives of people unless it happens to be necessary within their career. Most stakeholders felt that there were insufficient links forged between the world of work and business, and peoples' experience of ESD within schools. A key challenge for the future is to make sustainability something which people associate with the worlds of work and citizenship as much as the world of education.

Box 6.4. Innovation in Wales : Tir Gofal

The Tir Gofal agri-environmental scheme from CCW aims to help farmers maintain and enhance their farms, the agricultural landscape and its wildlife. One aspect of the scheme encourages farms to open up for educational visits from schools. In an era when most school children lead increasingly urban lives, this provides opportunities for them to experience and learn about the rural economy and way of life. This can help to demonstrate the applicability of sustainability principles to an important element of Welsh working life.

Conclusions

D ifferent regions have reached different stages of development in terms of ESD throughout Europe and beyond. Wales has an opportunity to share its emerging good practice with other regions, and to learn from innovative developments in countries such as Canada, Sweden and Denmark. Wales is one of the regions that, at a policy-making level, has really embraced the idea of integrating sustainable development throughout education. This is reflected in the words of Minister for Education and Lifelong Learning, Jane Davidson, when she wrote,

> *"Education for sustainable development and global citizenship is not an extra subject of study. It is a way of approaching the existing school curriculum and school life. It can be liberating for learners and teachers alike."* (ACCAC, 2002).

It is also evident in the work of the Assembly's ESD Advisory Panel whose work consistently emphasises the need to avoid a "bolt on" approach and the need to integrate ESD fully into all aspects of education within schools and colleges (and beyond).

Ten years ago, when writing about the challenge of integrating sustainable development issues into tertiary education, I highlighted two aspects which were similar to the problems that businesses faced in responding to sustainability concerns related to their products, productions systems or business strategies (Peattie, 1994). The first was a tendency towards *"end-of-pipe"* teaching, in which sustainability issues were "bolted-on" to conventional courses without the nature of the rest of the course, or other elements of the curriculum, being reconsidered from a sustainability perspective. This mirrors the tendency of companies often to "bolt-on" pollution reduction measures onto conventional production technologies rather than seeking to redesign them to reduce pollution at source. A related business concept is that of *"Best available technology, not entailing excessive cost"* (BATNEEC) which is enshrined within both UK and European environmental law. This concept allows business to plead "excessive cost" as a means to avoid having to use the best environmental technologies available within their industry. Education suffers from its own form of BATNEEC principle, which entails delivering *"best available teaching, not entailing excessive change"*.

In the context of UK education, such an approach is entirely understandable. The last ten years has witnessed a ceaseless succession of changes to the education system that has left teachers and those in education support and inspection desperate for some degree of stability and continuity. This has led to initiatives promoting ESD to stress the degree to which radical change is not required. For example,

"No radical overhaul of educational values, learning mechanisms, or core objectives is required to provide learning which facilitates sustainable development. In fact, ESD is likely to reinforce and promote key learning objectives and offers a new and invigorating way of approaching existing curricula and thinking about the world around us." (EAC, 2003).

This is perhaps wishful thinking. We know that the way that society has approached knowledge, technology and the environment in the past has created unsustainable development. Although education is nearly always proposed as a key solution to sustainability problems, it is also part of the problem. As Orr (1994) reminds us :

"It is worth noting that (the destruction of the planet) is not the work of ignorant people. Rather, it is largely the results of work by people with BAs, BScs, LLBs, MBAs, and PhDs".

Jucker (2002) points out that education is still shaped by an academic tradition that assumes that the general socio-economic status quo, although generally understood to be unsustainable in the long term, will largely be maintained. Without a more radical agenda for change, delivering ESD that helps to move us genuinely closer to sustainability will be difficult to achieve. Few in education seem to have an appetite for such radical change, or a belief that it is realistic to pursue.

In the short term, perhaps the key to enhancing ESD significantly, is not to position it as an issue that requires changes, but to ensure that it is a core component which is integrated into the many other educational changes that are ongoing and planned. At present the changes to *"Early years"* provision and the replacement of Key Stage 1 with the new *Foundation Curriculum* is a major set of changes in the primary sector. In the secondary sector, the provision for 14-19 year olds is also undergoing radical changes. These include a shift in the balance between traditional academic and more vocational courses, making the PSE curriculum compulsory and the development of new forms of educational partnerships. The *Learning the Sustainability Lesson* report (EAC, 2003) stresses that the current round of educational changes represents a *"tide that must be caught"*, in terms of seizing opportunities to integrate education and sustainable development. This is particularly true in Wales, where the new Welsh Baccalaureate qualification for the over 16s is also currently being piloted. On the basis of the pilot, a decision will be made as to whether it should be available to all students in Wales from 2006.

In considering the overall impact and value of ESD, it is important to put it back in the context of the total range of sources of knowledge and awareness about ESD included within Figure 6.1. The benefits of providing *"education for sustainable development"* which gives people the values, attitudes and skills to go out and contribute to the development of a more sustainable society are unquestionable. What is less certain, is whether we are complementing it sufficiently with *"education about sustainable development"* to give people a clear understanding of what sustainability is, what its components are and its relationship is to how they live.

One subject for discussion with all ESD stakeholders was the extent to which a consistent message about sustainable development as a coherent, if multi-faceted, whole was being communicated to people within Wales. The unanimous answer was that at present, it is not. Sustainable development was perceived as being presented to people in different ways at different times by a range of organisations. Sometimes it appeared to relate to the environment, sometimes it related to jobs, sometimes to communities and sometimes it was about other countries and the future. A metaphor for this situation is that the sustainable development concept is like a pyramid, it has distinctly different "faces", and the proportions of each face that are visible will depend upon the angle it is viewed from. From above, all three are equally represented, while from ground level only one may be visible. What needs to be communicated to people is a coherent vision of sustainable development as a whole so that they become familiar with the interconnection of the three "dimensions"; so that when one is visible, there is still awareness of the connection to the other two.

Various suggestions were made for encouraging this consistent and connected awareness of sustainability. One suggestion, which proved controversial, was seeking to use "branding" techniques to achieve the social marketing of sustainability within Welsh society. Many stakeholders recognised the potential power of branding, others thought it was impossible to apply effectively to as complex a concept as sustainability. Another was to produce a simple map of sustainability issues that could be used consistently across educational, economic and citizenship contexts. This could help to reinforce the concept of sustainability as including economic, social and environmental dimensions even when the specific issues under discussion related to only one of them. A suggested example of such as map is shown in Figure 6.2.

A recurrent theme when talking to stakeholders in ESD is the theme of resources. Many of the examples of good practice that exist in Wales, and elsewhere, do so because they are supported by goodwill and contributions which exceed the level at which projects have been resourced. Ultimately, those seeking to drive the ESD agenda forward are looking to secure additional resources to support it. These resources could fund a number of developments to promote ESD including:

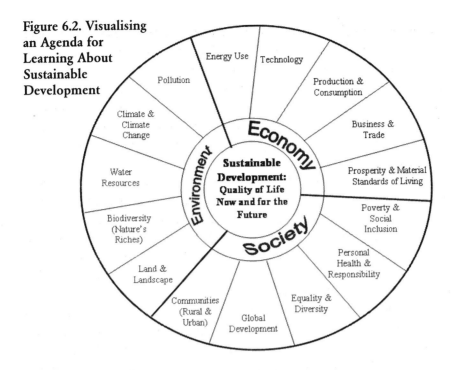

Figure 6.2. Visualising an Agenda for Learning About Sustainable Development

- Additional specialist educational support services within LEAs;
- Greater provision for school trips to support environmental, social and cultural learning;
- Investment in outdoor education facilities to accommodate more and larger environmental and social field trips. These could be integrated with eco-tourism ventures for example in terms of information materials, and used to attract school parties from other parts of the UK as well;
- Funding for the development of further educational resources including (a) resource packs to tackle key sustainability themes; (b) localised resources to support increased localisation of the ESD agenda; and (c) additional online and computer-based resources customised to support ESD within Wales.
- The extension of ESD within teacher training courses;
- Participation in ESD training as a contributor to teachers' pay progression;

Such an apparent "shopping list" might appear to be wishful thinking in a sector renowned for the tightness of budgets. However, a perspective which looks beyond the educational system may reveal both available finance and a compelling financial logic for making such investments. Landfill Tax money in Wales currently raises many millions of pounds. Its investment in ESD may make extreme good sense, since unless Wales improves participation rates in activities like recycling and composting, it will soon face punitive fines for failing to meet statutory EU targets. ESD provides some hope of explaining to children how and why the Welsh population need to become more engaged in recycling, and can also provide a channel to carry the message back into parental homes. Additional investment in ESD might appear to be an educational extravagance, but it may very soon be shown to represent a very shrewd financial investment.

Money is not the only resource that ESD must compete for. Competing for space and time in the curriculum is also a key barrier to further development. ESD struggles to compete with the time and effort dedicated to the key skills or numeracy, literacy and ICT skills. Sustainable development is also perceived as a more difficult area to demonstrate progress and to explain to parents when compared to these three areas.

One phrase recurred more than any other in this project's many interviews. That was the phrase *"If the Assembly Government is serious about ESD ...."*. This is not to say that stakeholders believed that the Assembly Government did not take the issue seriously. It more reflected concerns that although there is strong central support for ESD values, that in implementation, ESD will suffer the type of *"value-action gap"* that has hindered other elements of environmental policy (Blake, 1999). Ultimately many stakeholders felt that policy makers will need to go further in terms of investment in ESD, statutory provision for ESD in planning and inspection, and in coordinating many different elements of policy to reinforce the ESD message. If this can be achieved, then Wales has the potential to play a leading role in The United Nations' *"Decade of Education for Sustainable Development"* which begins in 2005.

References

ACCAC (2002) *Education for Sustainable Development and Global Citizenship*, ACCAC, Cardiff.

Bibbings, J. (2003) *Consumption in Wales: Encouraging the Sustainable Lifestyle*, Welsh Consumer Council, Cardiff

Blake, J. (1999) Overcoming the "value-action gap" in environmental policy: Tensions between National Policy and Local Experience, *Local Environment* (4), pp. 257-278

Coopey, J. (2001) Sustainable Development: A UK Business School Blind Spot?, *BAM News*, Winter 2001/2002, p. 12.

DETR (1999) *Sustainable Development Education Panel, First Annual Report 1998*, Department of Environment, Transport and the Regions, London.

DFE (1993) *Environmental Responsibility : an Agenda for Further and Higher Education (The Toyne Report)*, Department for Education, London.

EAC (2003) *Learning the Sustainability Lesson*, Environmental Audit Committee, London.

Jucker, R. (2002) Sustainability? Never Heard of It!: Some Basics We Shouldn't Ignore When Engaging In Education For Sustainability, *International Journal of Sustainability in Higher Education*, Volume 3 (1), pp. 8-18

MacNaghten, P. et al. (1995) *Public Perceptions and Sustainability in Lancashire: Indicators, Institutions, Participation*, Lancashire County Council and Lancaster University Centre for the Study of Environmental Change, Lancaster.

Peattie, K. (1994) A Green Light for Business Education?, *European Journal of Business Education*, Vol. 3 (2), pp. 39-47

Ofsted (2003) *Taking The First Step Forward: Towards An Education For sustainable development … A Guide To Good Practice In Primary And Secondary Schools*, Office for Standards in Education, London.

Orr, D.W. (1994), *Earth in Mind: On Education, Environment, and the Human Prospect*, Island Press, Washington, DC

SCAA (1996), *Teaching Environmental Matters through the National Curriculum*. The School Curriculum and Assessment Authority, London.

SDEP (2003), *Learning To Last : The Government's Sustainable Development Education Strategy For England*, Sustainable Development Education Panel, London.

SEC/ME (2001), *Greening Britain's schools : A study into the sustainability of our schools*, Southampton Environment Centre and Maverick Energy, Southampton.

UPSF (1995) *Environmental Responsibility – An Agenda for Tertiary Education*, The Tailloires Declaration of University Presidents for a Sustainable Future.

WCED (1987), *Our Common Future (The Brundtland Report)*, World Commission on Environment and Development, Oxford University Press, Oxford.

Chapter 7

Sustainable Futures

Martin Rhisiart

Introduction

Many governmental bodies in the European Union have used Futures and Foresight approaches in their policy-making processes. National Foresight programmes in the EU – and elsewhere in the world – have generally been based on long term industrial competitiveness objectives. Although there is no universal approach, most exercises have focused on ways of securing the success of those national economies over the longer term. Analyses of specific economic sectors, such as manufacturing, or technologies, such as nanotechnology and biotechnology, have been favoured topics for these exercises. Several European regions have also conducted Foresight exercises, with the majority focusing on competitiveness factors such as technology and innovation. In the main, neither national nor regional Foresight exercises have addressed Sustainable Development issues, although there are examples where governments have considered environmental factors. For example, while one of the topics for the latest UK Foresight programme has been flooding, the emphasis is placed on dealing with the socio-economic consequences of environmental problems.

Having an interest in Foresight/Futures and Sustainable Development, the OSKaR project team believed that there was considerable merit in exploring sustainable futures questions. Within the constraints of the project – especially time – it was important to build on the experiences and expertise of an external organisation. The Finland Futures Research Centre (FFRC) was asked to assemble a report that contained some of the principal trends affecting Sustainable Development – economic, social and environmental. The trends are generic in character and can be used for discussing policy issues in all European countries and regions. The principal task of this chapter will be to review some of the key economic, social and environmental trends affecting sustainable development. Three principal scenarios will be discussed in light of these trends. Further research and development of the sustainable futures agenda will be discussed in the final section of the chapter.

Economic and technological trends

Globalisation refers to 'a historical process which transforms the spatial organisation of social relations and transactions, generating transcontinental or inter-regional networks of interaction and the exercise of power' (Held and McGrew, 2002: 1-2). Globalisation is, according to one author, not a trend itself but the present world system (Friedman, 2000). There is certainly a strong evidence base to identify the economic processes of globalisation. Every country is involved in international trade, which has grown to unprecedented levels, both absolutely and in relation to national income. In 1999, world trade (merchandise and services) was valued at over $6.8 trillion, with exports having grown, as a percentage of world output, from 7.9 per cent in 1913 to 17.2 per cent in 1998 (Maddison, 2001; WTO, 2001).

Multinational corporations are dominant actors in transnational production. They account for about 25 per cent of world production and 70 per cent of world trade; their sales are equivalent to almost half of world GDP (UNCTAD, 2001). Although the majority of the multinationals' assets are typically located in OECD countries, the newly industrialising countries of East Asia and Latin America have become increasingly significant destinations for investment and an increasingly significant source of imports to OECD countries. By the end of the twentieth century, nearly 50 per cent of the world's total manufacturing jobs were located in developing economies, while over 60 per cent of the exports of developing countries to the developed world were manufactured goods, representing a twelve fold increase in less than four decades (UNDP, 1998). Global financial markets are another integral part of economic globalisation and international financial flows have grown exponentially in the last 30 years. Governance of economic globalisation is an important and contested issue. In the 1990s, developing countries were pressurised by the global institutions –International Monetary Fund (IMF), World Bank and World Trade Organisation (WTO) – and U.S. administrations to liberalise their economies. The results, in many cases, have caused enormous hardship and dislocation for the people in those countries and critics, who had an inside track in the decision-making processes, have pointed to erroneous analyses and misguided ideological zeal, particularly on the part of the IMF (Stiglitz, 2002). Economic globalisation, consisting of international trade, transnational production and international financial flows, is therefore certainly a major phenomenon affecting countries across the world.

Population growth is a topic that concerns a multitude of international non-governmental organisations (NGOs). In terms of regions of the globe, the picture varies considerably. Whereas there is a large measure of stability in the growth of populations in the more prosperous countries of the world, the population growth of East, Southeast and South Asia will have a major impact on global population growth, with all the challenges that it poses.

Figure 7.1. Population by World Region

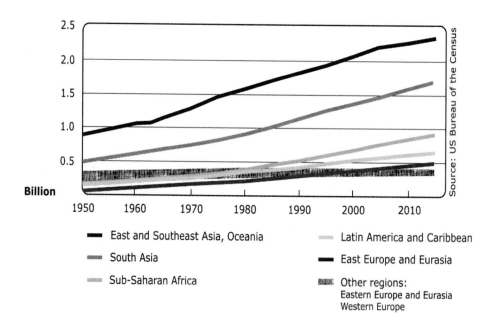

Economically, the trends also point to the 'turn of Asia'. It has been estimated that the GDP of East and Southeast Asia will be double that of Western Europe in 2015, having been at around the same level in 1990. Clearly, caution needs to be exercised in predicting outcomes. The 1997 East Asian crisis demonstrated that the global financial markets could cage the Asian 'tiger' economies. The inability of the international financial regime to manage the problems stimulated an important debate on future institutional frameworks. If the trends continue, it is possible that the strengthened position of the Asian economies will force a re-engineering of the framework of institutional rules that govern international finance.

Figure 7.2. GDP by World Region

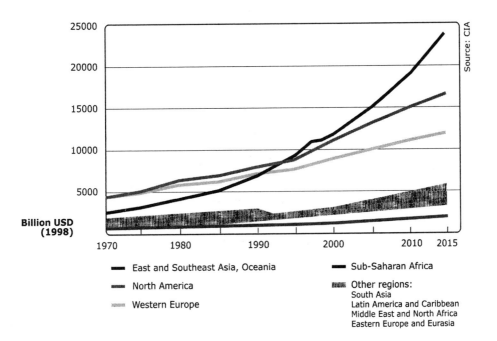

The restructuring of the Welsh economy over the last 25 years has been a reminder of the fallout created by economic globalisation. The collapse of the heavy industrial base posed severe policy challenges. Economically, the dominant paradigm that guided the post-industrial strategy of regenerating affected areas was the attraction of capital from overseas. Foreign direct investment (FDI) into Wales soared in the 1980s. Over the past two decades, Wales has been one of the biggest recipients of FDI in the European Union. Many of the investments took the form of branch plants of multinational manufacturing operations. While employment was created in the short term, the sustainability of such a strategy has been severely undermined by the loss of recent investments and the migration of jobs to lower cost economies. Labour costs in the newly industrialising economies and the developing countries are substantially lower than those in Wales and the Welsh experience reflects that of other developed countries in losing manufacturing employment to Southeast Asia. The EU Accession

Countries of Central and Eastern Europe have also supplanted countries such as Wales as prime recipients of FDI. Not only do they have lower wage economies, they are also on the verge of joining the large, single market for goods and services, which is the European Union. Although the outlook for manufacturing, in particular, generally appears bleak, the trends do point to some opportunities.

Future increases in the levels of prosperity in South and Southeast Asia suggest that there will be bigger markets and opportunities for companies in the developed world – as well as in the developing world – to exploit. Rather than merely accepting the inevitable flight of manufacturing industries to South and Southeast Asia, companies and policy-makers should consider how their products and services could be marketed to those countries. It also raises questions as to the role or competence of the Welsh economy in relation to the globalised picture. Adoption of new technologies and dematerialisation, discussed below, offer two positive routes.

It is important to emphasise that the 'the turn of Asia' – in population and economic terms – provides severe challenges to global sustainable development in addition to potential economic benefits to international trade. Consumption – and waste – patterns tend to reflect levels of economic well-being. The industrialised, prosperous countries have been responsible for a disproportionate amount of environmental pollution and their development paths have been based on carbon economies. If the industrialising countries emulate the past experiences of the developed or post-industrial countries, new and exacerbated environmental problems are likely to emerge. To an extent, many of the developed countries have started to re-orient economies towards more sustainable principles, as demonstrated in dematerialisation of those economies.

Dematerialisation of economic activity entails de-linking economic growth from the use of physical materials. Decreasing materials intensity means reducing the amount of material resource needed to produce the same outcome, de-linking material growth from economic growth. In other words we are getting more from less. Increasing materials intensity means the opposite: more resources are used for achieving the same economic outcome (re-linking). Although dematerialisation represents a relatively high level of eco-efficiency, it does not necessarily mean that the total use of natural resources is decreased. High rates of economic growth can counteract the effects of dematerialisation. In the 1980s, the trend in the EU-15 countries was towards weak re-linking of material flows (measured by domestic material extraction, DE). Since 1990, that trend has shifted towards strong de-linking (i.e. dematerialisation). The table below (Table 7.1) demonstrates that countries such as 'Belgium, Greece, Ireland, Portugal and Spain have performed weak re-linking during the whole period 1980-2000, showing again…a need of benchmarking policies for advancing sustainability in the EU' (Saloranta, 2003: 27).

Table 7.1. De- and re-linking process of material flows (domestic extraction, DE) in the EU member countries.

	1980–1990	1990–2000	1980–2000
Austria	Weak re-linking (A)	Strong de-linking (E)	Strong de-linking (E)
Belgium[1]	Weak re-linking (A)	Weak re-linking (A)	Weak re-linking (A)
Denmark	Imbalanced re-linking (A)	Strong de-linking (E)	Weak re-linking (A)
Finland	Weak re-linking (A)	Strong de-linking (E)	Weak re-linking (A)
France	Weak re-linking (A)	Strong de-linking (E)	Strong de-linking (E)
Germany	Strong de-linking (E)	Strong de-linking (E)	Strong de-linking (E)
Greece	Weak re-linking (A)	Weak re-linking (A)	Weak re-linking (A)
Ireland	Weak re-linking (A)	Weak re-linking (A)	Weak re-linking (A)
Italy	Weak re-linking (A)	Strong de-linking (E)	Strong de-linking (E)
Netherlands	Weak re-linking (A)	Strong de-linking (E)	Strong de-linking (E)
Portugal	Weak re-linking (A)	Weak re-linking (A)	Weak re-linking (A)
Spain	Weak re-linking (A)	Weak re-linking (A)	Weak re-linking (A)
Sweden	Weak re-linking (A)	Strong de-linking (E)	Weak re-linking (A)
UK	Weak re-linking (A)	Strong de-linking (E)	Weak re-linking (A)
EU-15	Weak re-linking (A)	Strong de-linking (E)	Strong de-linking (E)

1   Luxembourg included in the figures of Belgium.

A = Actual

E = Estimated

Science and technology will undergo rapid and dramatic changes over the next 25 years. The confluence and synergies of nanotechnology, biotechnology, information technology and cognitive sciences (NBIC) represent important new mergers between science and engineering, supported by governments and private investors. NBIC products will range from biometrics to restoring brain function and eye-sight. Over the next 25 years, NBIC approaches will integrate sciences, engineering, medicine, and business to change the very nature of R&D. Meanwhile, the risks of some new technologies and scientific developments are enormous, unprecedented, and, many argue, unpredictable. The risks are associated with unanticipated consequences of frontier research or applications and with new weapons applications.

Amaterialisation is a major, long-term economic trend and the trend in consumption is from material commodities to immaterial products and services (Saloranta, 2003: 28). Consumers in industrialised economies already have access to most basic commodities. The traditional utility value of products constitutes a decreasing proportion of the price, and 'the brand becomes the central object of consumption' (Saloranta, 2003: 28). Traditional social structures no longer dominate our way of looking at the world and culture compared with the past as consumers become aware of the plurality of cultures and the goods and 'signs' produced by them (Lash and Urry, 1994: 3). As goods become denuded of their material content, signs become increasingly important in their production. Lash and Urry distinguish between two categories of goods, according to their signs: the first group is post-industrial information products, whose content is predominantly cognitive, and the second is post-modern goods based on aesthetic content. The proportion of aesthetic content in the production of all goods increases as a result of the increased production of aesthetic goods (especially cultural goods) and the increasing importance of the aesthetic element in other products (design, brand building and other marketing) (Lash and Urry, 1994: 4).

Culture is a medium through which people construct and interpret the world they live in. Cultural phenomena and representations have been integrated into services and commodities for consumption. Economic competitiveness is therefore increasingly dependent on utilisation of cultural 'capital'. Creativity has been strongly associated with both cultural production and innovative economic production. One futurist believes that we are moving from an information society to a dream society (Jensen, 1999). According to Jensen's thesis, the highly rational information society, based on the production and processing of information, will give way to the dream society, in which the production of emotions and experiences will play an important role. In the dream society, storytellers will replace rational experts and consumers will purchase products that are associated with a good story, such as eggs produced by 'happy, free-range hens'. This reinforces the point that consumption in many Western societies is based more on personal values and lifestyle than satisfying basic needs. Turning attention to the Welsh context, one question is clear: how can the economy gain from such trends?

It it is important to emphasise that notions of cultural production should not be confused with the Welsh and English languages, although there are important dimensions to the cultures that are associated with the languages. In interpreting these trends, two complementary options can be identified for the Welsh economy: cultural capital that is specific to Wales, and that which is generic. First, many factors have an impact on culture and its manifestation, including history, natural environment, heritage, built environment and climate. In other words, it is the combination of phenomena and features which constitute the uniqueness of Wales (or any other country). Culture-based tourism, for example, has been identified as a potentially lucrative sector. It relates to overt notions of 'traditional' culture, such as literature. Its significance extends beyond the focus on a particular author or poet as it incorporates various cultural signs and values, such as romanticism, self-reliance, solidarity and a sense of belonging. One measure of successful Welsh companies in the future will be their capacity to utilise cultural capital and infuse products and services with values and signs. To achieve that goal, companies will need a diverse set of skills, with a particular emphasis on marketing, economic and social intelligence and creativity tools. Second, companies will need to be alert to the opportunities presented in international markets by the dream society. The emphasis here will not be on identification with a particular spatial-social context. Rather, it will be on generic cultural values (e.g. products and services produced according to certain ethical standards).

Social trends

The preceding discussion on the changing patterns and values of consumers points to the complex relationship between social changes and economic consequences. In this section, a selection of important social trends will be discussed. The Information Society has been used as the label to capture the dominant social and economic model of the late twentieth century. Inevitably, as soon as one model becomes established and becomes part of the common vernacular, inquisitive minds begin focusing on the model that will succeed the existing one. Thus the Information Society will be replaced by a Network Society, based on services and stories:

Industrial logic, the operational mode for the industrial society, is being replaced by a new model, the logic of networks, in which production is predominantly based on services. This transition has its roots in fundamental changes in technological infrastructure, working life, markets and habits of consumption, values, and perhaps, most significantly, our relationship to natural resources. (Saloranta, 2003: 38).

The Network Society challenges all previous modes of operation, posing the question: 'how can we do things differently?'

Figure 7.3. Industrial Society, Information Society and Network Society

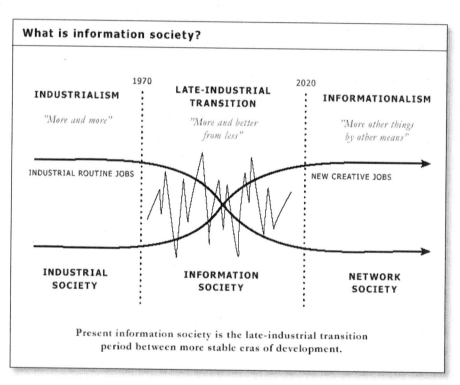

Malaska / Wilenius 1996, 2003 quoted in Saloranta, 2003

Population growth has already been cited as a major challenge for the 21st century. Although the rate of population growth is slowing down (Figure 7.4), the increase in the absolute numbers will create a serious demand on natural resources (Figure 7.5). Urbanisation is another significant trend. Providing nutrition, shelter, water and sanitation will be a great challenge, failure to meet which might result in increased migrations, diseases and conflicts.

Figure 7.4. World Annual Population Change

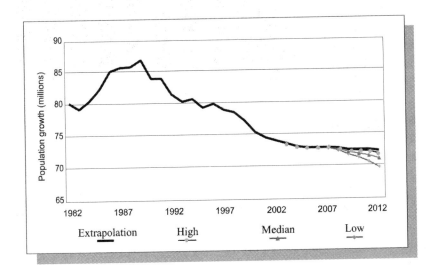

There is no population growth in Western Europe. That is not to say that the countries of Western Europe are immune to many of the consequences of population growth. International instability and crises may occur as a result of population growth and there are already examples of the impact of such patterns on western countries. In particular, conflicts generate high numbers of refugees and governments often have difficulties in managing sudden influxes.

Figure 7.5. Global population

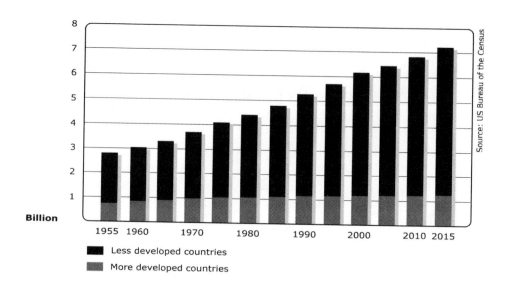

Source: US Bureau of the Census

A number of experts have sought to explain socio-economic phenomena by analysing the cultural values of individuals within a spatial and temporal context. One systematic approach has produced a cultural map of the world (Inglehart, 1997; Inglehart, Basañez and Moreno, 1998). It is based on the responses to scores on questions concerning political, religious, sexual and economic norms, given for the 1990-93 World Values Survey by more than 60,000 respondents in 43 societies. The dimension of traditional vs. secular rational authority reflects the degree of traditional authority (usually religious), adherence to family and communal obligations and norms of sharing. The opposing position is secular authority, which is legitimated by rational-legal norms. The other dimension, survival vs. well-being, captures the status of post-industrial societies, where the emergence of unprecedented levels of wealth and the welfare states has given rise to a shift from scarcity norms, emphasising hard work and denial. The opposing position, well-being, consists of postmodern values that emphasise quality of life, emancipation of women and sexual minorities, and self-expression.

Figure 7.6. Inglehart's cultural map of the world

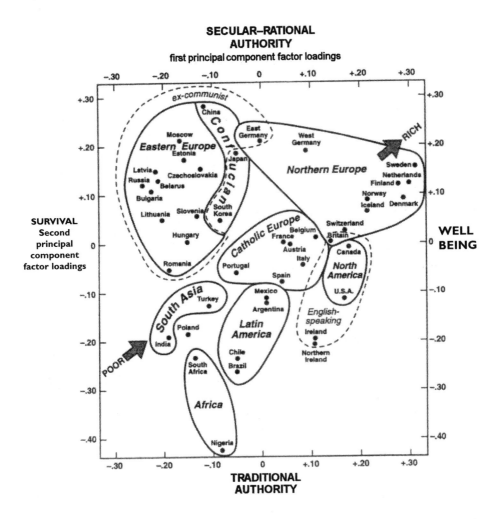

Another author argues that a new class has emerged in the new economy (Florida, 2002). Job profile is the defining feature of the class: at its core are people working in science and engineering, architecture and design, education, arts, music and entertainment. The economic function of the new class is to produce new ideas, technologies and content. A broader group of professionals surrounds the core, including creative professionals in business, law, finance and healthcare. Although there is a cross-section of professions represented by the class, Florida argues that it is their cultural values and lifestyle preferences that bind the group together. Creativity, individuality and merit are the group's core values. In the United States, there are approximately 50 million 'culturally creative' people who value social activism, concern for the environment, self-improvement and spirituality. One of the central ideas of the theory is that the creative class gravitates towards creative environments. A corollary is that companies must re-locate to where the creative class lives. This is sharply at odds with the traditional notion of people having to relocate to where the employment exists. While it is important to ensure that creative environments are nurtured, it is also important to avoid brain drain. Development is very often imbalanced – and unsustainable – when highly skilled individuals migrate to economic hotspots. Governments should certainly avoid being accomplices in the process.

The digital divide is the term used to denote inequality and marginalisation within the information society. It contains three key facets: (1) a lack of penetration of technological innovation in the information society, (2) utilisation of the Internet, and (3) the extent to which use of the Internet and ICT contributes to users' welfare and quality of life. Overcoming the digital divide means achieving digital literacy, which, in turn, depends on three core elements: motivation, access and skills. Knowledge and opportunities in the information society can often be lost unless motivation, access and skills are present.

Environmental Trends

The Intergovernmental Panel on Climate Change (IPCC) announced in 1995 that the great majority of evidence points to human activity as the source of climate change. In its Third Assessment Report, published in 2001, the IPCC states that the latest research has confirmed the significant role of anthropogenic climate change, especially over the latter half of the twentieth century. According to the IPCC, the surface temperatures of the Earth have increased by 0.4 – 0.8 degrees centigrade since the mid-19th century. At the same time, the carbon dioxide content of the atmosphere has risen by 31 per cent, and that of methane by 151 per cent. The concentrations are higher than at any point over the last 420,000 years. It is estimated that the doubled CO_2 concentration will increase the global mean temperature by 1.5 – 4.5 degrees centigrade. If the concentrations increase further, the temperature will continue to increase. The increase will be least in areas near the equator and greatest in the polar areas. Global precipitation will increase, but so will evaporation. The increase in evaporation will be greater over continents than oceans, and landmasses in the temperate zones, in particular, are expected to be dry in the summer and wet in winter. A warmer atmosphere retains more moisture, which increases the magnitude of thunderstorms locally. The greater volume of water and the melting of mountain glaciers will lead to increases in sea levels. Melting of the ice caps has already been observed and if the warming continues at the current rate, the sea level could rise by several metres over the coming centuries (IPCC, 2001).

Table 7.2. Impacts of climate change on ecosystems: People

Climate change affects areas where people are already living in dire straits. Although climate change may be of benefit to some areas, the disadvantages to other areas can be catastrophic.

Water and food

- Although higher carbon dioxide levels initially increase the productivity of plants, increased drought eliminates this benefit from large areas in Sub-Saharan Africa and in South and South East Asia. Food production in China also suffers from climate change.

- A warming climate increases the size of dry areas and deserts, making increasing areas impossible to cultivate. The rise in the sea level also threatens to make fields uncultivable, especially in Asia.

- 60–350 million people are threatened with famine if carbon dioxide concentrations double and population growth continues at present rate. The growing shortage of food is caused by climate change; a total of 600–900 million people will be threatened with famine in the mid-21st century.

- Increasing evaporation may decrease the volume of the Nile by 11% and that of the Indus by as much as 43%.

- Problems in food production may lead to conflicts in areas where the water used for food production comes from the territory of another state.

- It is also estimated that climate warming will push fertile agricultural areas to the north. Food sufficiency will thus require increased distribution of food between different geographic areas. China, India and Africa in particular are in a critical position, because food production is declining in these densely populated areas.

- Access to water in a warmer climate will become very difficult in many areas, including Kuwait, Jordan, Israel, Rwanda, Somalia, Algeria, Libya, Egypt, South Africa, Iran and Ethiopia.

Table 7.2. Impacts of climate change on ecosystems: People (continued)

Infectious diseases and storms

- Climate warming will increase the distribution of infectious diseases such as malaria, dengue fever, cholera, salmonella, yellow fever and hanta virus, as well as the prevalence of deaths and coronary diseases caused by heat waves.

- If the climate warms by 3–5 degrees in a hundred years, in the latter half of the 21st century 60% of the world's population will become susceptible to malaria instead of the current 45%. It is expected that malaria will also be encountered further north in Europe.

- In 1998, storms killed more people than in 200 years. The reason was Hurricane Mitch, which hit Midwest America in late November. The season's storms caused USD 3.2 billion worth of insurance damages in the USA.

- The expansion of warm ocean areas will increase the damage caused by storms; the most powerful storms can already achieve their maximum speed over the ocean before making landfall when they lose their power.

- The probability of floods and landslides will grow as the climate warms, especially in temperate and humid areas.

- Rainstorms will increase the risk of landslides. Landslides are an extremely big threat in areas where buildings are situated on hillsides. For example, rainstorms and floods killed about 30,000 people in December 1999 in Venezuela.

- According to The Reinsurance Association of America, damages paid by the company have grown in the USA in direct proportion to the number of large-scale storms.

- Hurricane Andrew in 1992 cost USD 16 billion in damages, driving seven insurance companies to bankruptcy. Some of the cost comes from the cessation of business operations – 40% of the damages caused by Hurricane Hugo came from this.

- On the other hand, we can say that the increased value of insured property (increased amount of population and property) and increased construction in areas susceptible to storms are at least as important explanatory factors as the increased amount of insurance damages.

Table 7.2. Impacts of climate change on ecosystems: People (continued)

Rising sea level

- The IPCC has estimated that over the next hundred years the sea level will rise by about 10–90 cm. The rising sea level threatens large areas of low-lying land. It is estimated that about half the Earth's population lives in coastal areas, which are often fertile arable land as well. The rise of sea level will increase coastal erosion and thereby destroy land areas. According to one estimate, a rise of one metre per hundred years would force about a billion people to relocate, taking population growth into account.

- A rise of one metre would flood 6% of the land area of Netherlands, 17% of Bangladesh, and as much as 80% of the Majuro atoll in the Marshall Islands. Tens of millions of Bangladeshis would be forced to migrate or live in extremely poor conditions. There are populous and low-lying coastal areas also in Nigeria, Sierra Leone, Cameroon and Angola. Furthermore, there are an increasing number of coastal cities in the world, where the rising sea level will have a great impact. For example, the industrial city of Lagos on the Nigerian coast and Dar es Salaam in Tanzania are already threatened by the rising sea level and subsequent erosion. It is estimated that the problems of these cities will have a great impact on the economic development of these countries.

- The rise of the sea level and floods caused by storms can push salt water far inland, obstructing artificial irrigation and making arable land saline, especially in South, East and South East Asian rice cultivation areas. The rise in the sea level would endanger the food supply of as much as 200 million people.

- At present, about 46 million people suffer from damage caused by storms. If the sea level should rise by one metre, floods would affect the lives of 118 million people.

Multiple Sources (Saloranta, 2003)

Table 7.3. Impacts of climate change on ecosystems: Animals

- As a result of an increase of just two degrees, in certain northern boreal forests 10–15% of all species will become extinct.
- If warmer springs move the schedule of procreation of insects or fish, this may lead to mass deaths among migratory birds and land animals.
- Floods and the resultant changes in the water ecosystems of rivers can be a threat to migratory fish.
- The warming of rivers is expected to lead to the destruction of entire habitats of cold-water fish, such as salmon.
- The amount of zoo plankton on the west coast of the United States has dropped by 70% as the result of warm water preventing colder and more nutritious water from rising to the surface. Also the forests of algae have become consistently smaller and biologically poorer.
- As a result, fish catches have become smaller and the number of seabirds in the Gulf of California has dropped by 90% since the counts began in 1987.
- Melting icebergs in the Arctic Ocean threaten algae living on the underside of the ice, which provide food for fish and birds and affect whales and seals. It is expected that populations of species dependent on icebergs, such as polar bear and walrus, will decline.
- Mountain species suffer as their habitats get smaller.
- Warming of the oceans by only 1–2 degrees leads to the death of corals, or to the bleaching of coral, and a rise of 3–4 degrees to the destruction of the entire reef. A rapid rise in the sea level could also pose a threat to corals, which live only in shallow waters.
- It is estimated that 65% of all ocean fish species depend on corals at some point in their life.
- Warming has already caused untold damage to the coral reefs of the world, scientists announced in an international conference in March 1998. The destruction of coral reefs may have serious consequences for the livelihood of millions of people, they warned.
- Damage to coral reefs in 1998 was wider than ever before. Their impact on biodiversity, fishing and tourism are considerable. In some parts of the Indian Ocean, mortality is up to 90% and shallow reefs in the Maldives, Sri Lanka, Kenya and Tanzania have been almost totally destroyed. Also coral reefs in South East Asia have suffered great damage.

Multiple Sources (Saloranta, 2003)

Table 7.4. Impacts of climate change on ecosystems: Plants

- Photosynthesis starts a week earlier in the spring than 30 years ago.
- Plant species are moving to higher altitudes in the Swiss and Austrian Alps, where temperatures have risen 0.7 degrees during the past hundred years.
- A change of 1–3.5 degrees in a hundred years moves the temperature zones of the earth some 150–550 km towards the poles. For example, the rate of migration of trees has been estimated to be normally 4–200 km in a hundred years.
- Entire animal species may change their migration patterns and distribution.
- Dry regions, bush lands and savannahs will become drier, in addition to which wetlands and marshes in the dry regions will suffer. For example, it is estimated that 85% of wetlands in Spain and Greece will dry out because of climate change. Forest fires will also become more frequent in the Mediterranean area.
- The northern boreal zone is expected to encroach slowly on the Arctic tundra and species adapted to the tundra will decline, because maritime areas in the north limit the suitable habitats.
- Southern pests and plant diseases will spread towards the north, because the cold winter will no longer restrict them as much as it used to.
- Wetlands will dry out both in the hottest areas and in the Arctic zone, where the thawing of permafrost will create flood lakes. At the same time, the specialised flora and fauna of wetlands will lose their habitats and face extinction.
- The natural carbon binding ability of peatlands diminishes as the peatlands dry up. Dry peatlands may even turn into sources of carbon, contributing to the escalation of climate change. On the other hand, drying peatlands makes for smaller methane emissions.
- The rise in sea level threatens coastal wetlands, deltas and mangrove forests which house a great biological diversity. Even at the present rate, the rising sea level may destroy these areas by 0.5–1.5% annually.
- At the present rate, the sea may cover as much as half the coastal wetlands within the next century. Moving coastal wetland ecosystems with the coastal zone is made more difficult by dense human habitation along the coasts.
- Droughts increase the likelihood of forest fires in temperate, subtropical and partly also in tropical areas. Forest fires will increase especially in areas where forests have become drier because of insect or felling.
- Forest fires release enormous amounts of carbon into the atmosphere and speed up the extinction of species. Particularly significant in this respect are tropical forests, which have more species per hectare than anywhere else in the world.

Multiple Sources (Saloranta, 2003)

The Living Planet Index is calculated as the average of three separate indices relating to the abundance of forest, freshwater and marine species. The index shows an overall decline of about 37 per cent between 1970 and 2000. The forest species population index is a measure of the trends in populations of 282 bird, mammal and reptile species living in forest ecosystems around the world. The freshwater index comprises populations of 195 species of birds, mammals, reptiles, amphibians and fish from lakes, rivers and wetland ecosystems. The marine index includes 217 bird, mammal, reptile and fish species found in marine and coastal ecosystems. Between 1970 and 2000, terrestrial species populations declined by about 15 per cent on average, marine populations declined by about 35 per cent, and freshwater species declined by by about 54 per cent (WWF, 2002). Of the factors that cause species population decline, 85.2 per cent are caused by human activity. Such a situation is, by definition, unsustainable for biodiversity. Even the publicity generated by the loss of species has failed to reverse these trends.

Table 7.5. Population decline threat factors and their relative weights (source: WWF)

- Forestry 30.2%
    * forest management activities 6.8%
    * changes in tree species composition 7.1%
    * changes in age structure of forests 5.4%
    * reduction of decaying wood 10.9%
- Overgrowth of open habitats 27.5%
- Extremely small population or habitat 11%
- Construction 10.5%
- Chemical disturbances 4.0%
- Construction of waterways 3.9%
- Ditching and peatland drainage 3.5%
- Mining, sand and gravel quarrying 2.1%
- Mechanical wear 2.0%
- Extreme fluctuations in population size 1%
- Changes in arable land 0.9%
- Hunting and collecting 0.6%
- Other known factors 1.6%
- Unknown factors 1.2%

Table 7.5. Population decline threat factors and their relative weights (source: WWF) (continued)

> Of the factors, 85.2% are directly caused by human activity. The greatest single factors are commercial forest management, overgrowing of open habitats, and construction. As we may assume that all these factors will only increase with the growing human population and economic growth, the depletion of species will escalate in the near future under the 'business as usual' approach. Thus, the diversity of the biosphere will continue to decline in the foreseeable future.

Water tables are falling on every continent. About 40 per cent of the world population lives in the 260 major international water basins shared by more than two countries. Agriculture accounts for 70 per cent of all human usage of fresh water and according to the Food and Agriculture Organisation (FAO), water for agriculture needs to increase by 60 per cent to feed an additional 2 billion people by 2030 (quoted in Saloranta, 2003). Water is not a problem in most of Western Europe. Southern Europe has some problems whereas Northern and Central Europe are reasonably well off. Water has been a highly politicised issue in Wales for some time. Given some of the scarcity and supply problems highlight, it might continue to be a contentious issue in years to come.

Scenarios for Wales

The preceding sections have outlined some of the principal trends affecting sustainable development. These trends present policy-makers – and society as a whole – with challenges and fundamental choices. Three broad scenarios exist for development. The first two are based on the growth of material production and material consumption. In the first, the development trajectory of material consumption results in pollution and the depletion of natural resources. Ultimately, the capacity of growth is exhausted and there is possible systemic collapse. The second scenario mirrors the material consumption of the first but produces better socio-economic consequences in terms of higher standards of living and technological development. Historically, the development model of Wales has led to significant pollution and depletion of natural resources without, in many cases, higher standards of living and technological development. The Welsh Index of Multiple Deprivation (NAW, 2000) assesses the 865 electoral divisions of Wales according to six domains: income, employment, health, education, housing and access. The Index demonstrates that there is a big gap between the most deprived and the least deprived communities of Wales. It also demonstrates that there is significant variation within Local Authorities.

Figure 7.7. Trends: the general choice of path

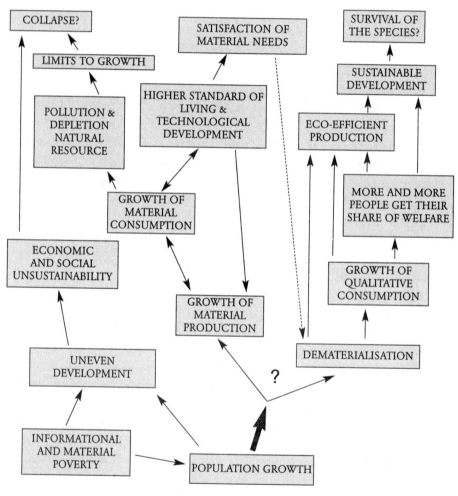

(Saloranta, 2003)

Although there are inequalities of wealth in Wales, in the global context of course, standards of living are high and there is quite a widespread satisfaction of material needs. With the satisfaction of material needs, the socio-economic trends discussed in previous sections point to a movement towards dematerialisation. Shifting a country from one scenario or development path to another is not achieved by a whim. Much of the impetus originates in socio-economic trends across different countries and the choices taken by individuals and companies. However, governments do have scope to influence such trends, and indeed, effect sustainable outcomes, particularly by shaping the structure in which those choices are made. The public sector in Wales has four main roles to play in facilitating this change.

- The public sector can directly influence the behaviour of companies through its procurement practices. The public sector in Wales operates under the framework of the European Union, which is strict in its anti-competitive legislation. However, several examples exist where EU countries and regions pursue a more creative public procurement strategy. This requires strong political will and a determination to make it happen.
- In addition to stimulating sustainable practices through procurement, the public sector needs to lead by example and demonstrate its own commitment to sustainability through tangible actions.
- Education and information is essential to foster a bottom-up approach to sustainability. The public sector needs to inform the general public of the importance of acting sustainably through marketing campaigns. Core sustainability values such as citizenship and responsibility need to be promoted in addition to the benefits of sustainable consumption.
- The public sector can reward companies that act sustainably and which develop sustainable products and services. There is a well-established business support environment in Wales, populated by a plethora of organisations. A range of mechanisms can be applied to ensure that the public sector only supports companies that either already operated sustainably or are willing to take steps to do so.

Conclusion

It is clear from this review of economic, social and environmental trends that countries and regions face significant challenges in achieving development that is sustainable. These trends are generic and are applicable to many countries. Use of such trends is important in mapping development trajectories and if Wales is to move towards a more sustainable trajectory, it needs a solid information base from which it can make decisions. Current use of trends and scenarios tends to be on an ad hoc basis. A dedicated resource that is focused on sustainable development trends and scenarios would be extremely beneficial for policy-making and analysis.

Governments and societies face fundamental choices. Government practice needs to provide incentives for sustainable actions as well as sanctions against unsustainable actions. Only by challenging basic, unsustainable assumptions and actions will people grasp the importance of acting in a sustainable and responsible way. Choosing the dematerialisation path is the only viable option but it needs to be accompanied by broader social processes. Harnessing the cultural capital of Wales will be a critical factor in generating wealth, creating social equity and vibrancy, and protecting the environment.

References

Florida, R. (2002) *The Rise of the Creative Class – and How it's Transforming Work, Leisure, Community and Everyday Life*, Basic Books, New York.

Friedman, T. (2000) *The Lexus and the Olive Tree*, Anchor, New York.

Held, D. and McGrew, A. (eds.) (2002) *Governing Globalization. Power, Authority and Global Governance*, Polity, Cambridge

Inglehart, R. (1997) *Modernization and Postmodernization: Cultural, Economic and Political Change in 43 Societies*, Princeton University Press, Princeton

Inglehart, R., Basañez, M. and Moreno, A. (1998) *Human values and beliefs. A cross-cultural sourcebook. Political, religious, sexual and economic norms in 43 societies*, University of Michigan Press, Ann Arbor

IPCC (2001) *Climate Change 2001: Synthesis report.* http://www.ipcc.ch/pub/reports.htm

Jensen, R. (1999) *The Dream Society. How the Coming Shift from Information to Imagination Will Transform your Business.* McGraw-Hill, New York

Lash, S. and Urry, J. (1994) *Economies of Signs and Space*, Sage, London

Maddison, A. (2001) *The World Economy: A Millennial Perspective*, OECD, Paris

National Assembly for Wales (2000) Welsh Index of Multiple Deprivation, http://www.wales.gov.uk/keypubstatisticsforwales/content/publication/social/2000/depri vation/intro_e.htm

Saloranta, P. (2003) *Sustainable Development Trends*, Report to the OSKaR Project. FFRC, Helsinki

Stiglitz, J. (2002) *Globalization and its Discontents*, Penguin, London

UNCTAD (2001) *World Investment Report*, UNCTAD, Geneva

UNDP (1998) *Globalization and Liberalization*, UNDP, New York

UNEP (2002) *Global Environment Outlook 3*. http://www.unep.org/geo/geo3/english/pdf.htm

WTO (2001) *World Trade Report*, World Trade Organisation, Geneva

WWF (2002)*The Living Planet Report*.
        http://www.panda.org/downloads/general/LPR_2002.pdf

Chapter 8

Policy Lessons for Implementing Sustainable Development in Wales

Martin Rhisiart and Meirion Thomas

Deriving policy lessons

A s discussed in the Introduction (Chapter 1), the TASK programme has been piloting a number of approaches to sustainable development. All four of the actions described have had discrete roles to play and specific outputs to deliver. At a strategic level, the TASK programme has been charged with producing lessons that can be used to operationalise sustainable development principles into mainstream policy-making. The Observatory – or OSKaR project – had the formal leadership for devising and managing this learning process.

The policy learning framework (Figure 8.1) was constructed by the Observatory as a heuristic device to provide a central focus for all of the projects. On the right hand side, there are operational and project lessons that relate to the four individual projects.

- Operational lessons represent new understanding and knowledge relating to the different kinds of instruments used. For example, each project will have experiences of the use of media and other instruments to communicate their activities.
- Project lessons might include insights into institutional structures that are required to deliver the project successfully.

On the left hand side of Figure 8.1 are the policy lessons. Four main areas are listed in which the programme is seeking to learn policy lessons:

Figure 8.1 Deriving Policy Lessons

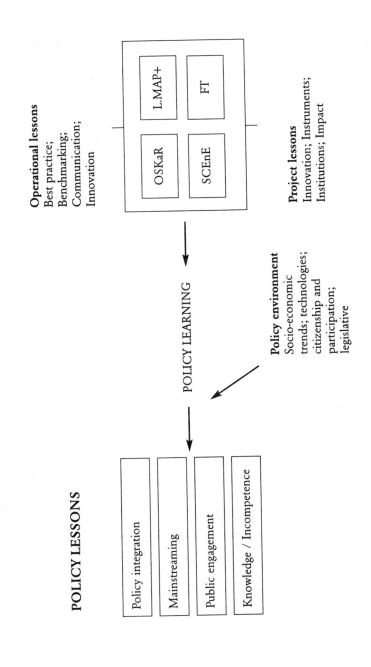

- Mainstreaming: the process by which the principles of sustainability, as demonstrated within the set of experimental approaches – can become the basis for wider, conventional policy-making;
- Public engagement: how innovative approaches to sustainable development can engage with citizens;
- Increased knowledge and competence: the ways in which actors in the policy-making system can acquire and use new knowledge relating to sustainable development;
- Policy integration: how vertical and horizontal structures – and practices – need to take account of a policy priority (i.e. SD) that cuts across traditional functional areas of operation.

The policy lessons – and indeed the whole framework – are influenced by the trends, structures and drivers of the policy environment. A number of the most relevant trends have already been discussed in Chapter 7. The principal drivers that are featured in the framework are:

- Legislative framework: the constitutional rules and formal processes that guide policy-making within a multi-governance context;
- Socio-economic trends: current and likely future trends which will have significant consequences in the way societies and economies develop;
- Technological developments: the pace of change and the disruptive nature of new technologies which will pose new challenges to citizens and policy-makers;
- Citizenship and participation: the way in which individuals relate to society and governments which will impact on the efficacy and delivery of common goods.

'Learning by doing' was a core principle for the TASK programme from the outset. As more material and messages have emerged from the projects, it has been possible to construct a broader model for the policy learning process within the programme.

The projects individually have generated new knowledge relating to various aspects of sustainability. Many areas of this new knowledge were applied, disseminated and tested through channels such as the debates, technology symposia and sounding boards. Comments received through those consultative channels produced a feedback mechanism, typically leading to an improved understanding of the sustainability issues discussed – particularly from am implementation perspective.

In addition to research work, the Observatory used two principal mechanisms to advance the policy learning process: symposia and debates. Representatives from each

Figure 8.2 Model of the Learning Process

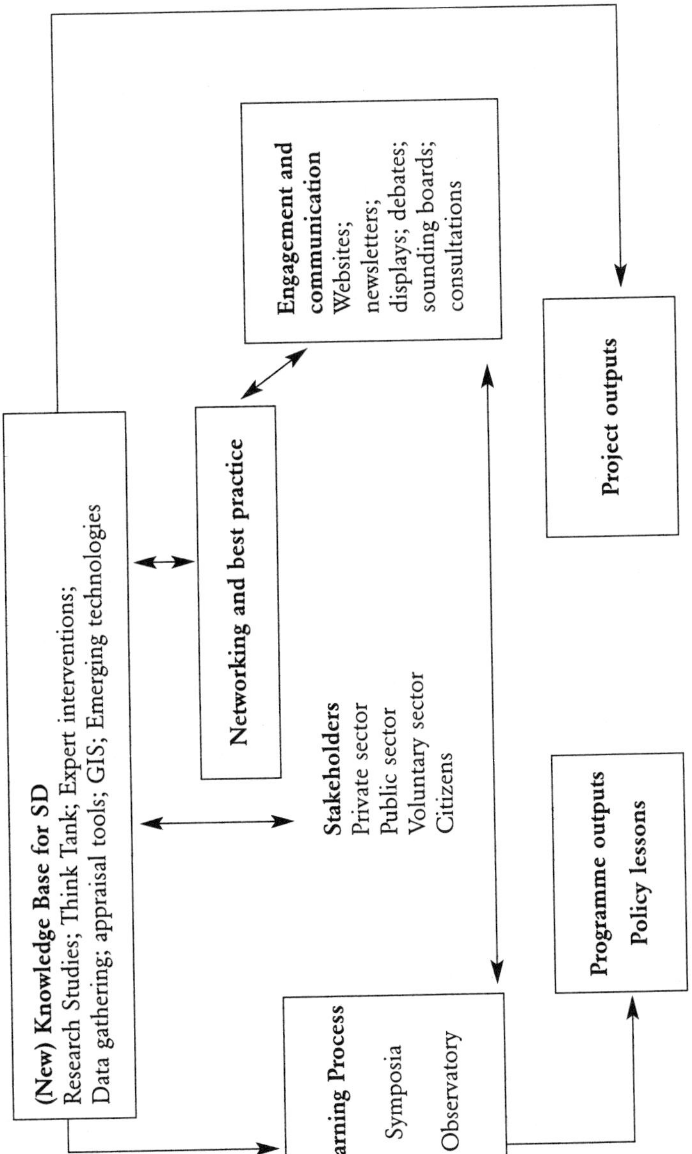

(New) Knowledge Base for SD
Research Studies; Think Tank; Expert interventions;
Data gathering; appraisal tools; GIS; Emerging technologies

Networking and best practice

Engagement and communication
Websites;
newsletters;
displays; debates;
sounding boards;
consultations

Stakeholders
Private sector
Public sector
Voluntary sector
Citizens

Learning Process
Symposia
Observatory

Project outputs

Programme outputs
Policy lessons

project participated in programme symposia to identify and discuss issues that emerged from their activities. The symposia were designed as an iterative process; many of the issues identified were re-visited and re-evaluated in subsequent symposia in light of new knowledge and experience. Another input, which was deemed vital, was the engagement of a cross-section of stakeholders that were interested in sustainability issues. A series of regional debates was organised, whose main aims were to:

- Solicit the views of a range of stakeholders in Wales on a number of important questions;
- Stimulate dialogue and networking between actors involved in each geographical area;
- Validate the lessons emerging from the TASK programme as a whole.

Over 200 people, representing a broad cross-section of organisations attended the debates. The exercise achieved its main aim of soliciting the views of civil society on key sustainable development considerations.

Policy lessons

This section presents some of the main policy lessons identified by the Observatory in its programme of research, symposia and debates.

Implementing policy at the regional level

The opportunity offered by the successful implementation of sustainable development at a regional level is an opportunity that not all regions or regional governments will be able to grasp. As Flynn and Morgan (Chapter 2) point out "while sustainable development policy is largely *designed* at the national and supra-national scales, it is actually *delivered* at the sub-national scales". Cohen (Chapter 5) points out that the regional level can make a significant contribution in addressing the challenges of waste. These benefits are unlikely to be restricted to the region in question. Indeed, the prize for a successful sustainable development based region is likely to be manifested on at least two levels – the local and the global. The implementation of successful local sustainable development policies will give clear benefits in the key areas of society, economic and environmental life. At the global level, the first strongly sustainable development regions will be seen as pacesetters for a considerable time and this could provide a completely fresh impetus to the well-being of the region, resulting in significantly new and different life choices for its population. However, as Rhisiart (Chapter

7) concludes, the scenarios that may provide the context for sustainable development present policy-makers with significant challenges and fundamental choices. Rhisiart reminds us that shifting a country from one scenario or development path to another is not achieved by a whim. This is even more the case for a region that, by the nature of the global governance that affects sustainable development policy, may have only partial control over the policy prescriptions that it may be able to apply.

The primary responsibility for implementing sustainable development at a regional level clearly falls to the regional government, in the case of Wales, the National Assembly for Wales. This is a challenging and ambitious task and it is only the government that has the competence and the electoral mandate to take on the task. Peattie (Chapter 6) suggests that a key test of the success of a sustainable development agenda will be whether a society can develop a strong base of sustainability knowledge. Cohen (Chapter 5) refers to the allocation of power at the regional level and distinguishes between the two types of policy development that it entails: capacity building and integration. As Morgan and Morley (Chapter 3) point out in relation to food – but it equally applies generally – in terms of public policy, implementing sustainable development is a radical and unique enterprise. One of the key lessons from the OSKaR research is that, although local government is the key administrative tier responsible for the delivery of sustainable development, the policy itself and the leadership behind the policy is the responsibility of the regional government as part of its commitment to sustainable development. Indeed, it appears that many operating in local authorities, as well as at the community and voluntary level, believe that Sustainable Development is practised at the local level, in spite of, not because of the policy makers.

This rather negative or sceptical view is illustrated by the feeling in a number of areas of this book that the research and policy learning has revealed a general assumption that 'when the chips are down' sustainable development will be at risk from the inevitable short-termism of government and the attraction of politicians to so-called 'quick-fixes'. In illustration of this scepticism, the debates carried out by the Cardiff Business School team as part of the TASK programme revealed that the timescale of the impact of sustainable development is expected to be a key factor in implementing sustainable development at a regional level. Similarly Flynn and Morgan (Chapter 2) refer to an attitude amongst Assembly officials of "cherry picking" of policy areas where progress can most easily be made. The example of waste was frequently given as a short term problem with, relatively, quick and easy answers, therefore action will be taken. This is in contrast to global warming, which is a long term problem with only long term solutions so there is assumed to be little incentive for short-termist politicians and policy makers at a regional government level to take action.

There is however, an understanding of the difficulties faced by policy makers and politicians in attempting to implement sustainable development. For example, the funding cycles and associated output targets and measurements under which national governments, and therefore regional administrations, operate are recognised as potential barriers to sustainable development action. In the Welsh context, a number of the authors in this book (for example, Flynn and Morgan in Chapter 2 and Cohen in Chapter 5) have intimated, and this is supported by the Cardiff Business School debates, that there is actually no shortage of policy from the Welsh Assembly Government and that therefore actual new policy making is not the main issue for sustainable development in Wales. What is needed however is that the National Assembly for Wales and the Welsh Assembly Government show a consistency in both the policy and the resource allocation for sustainable development.

A significant feature of the research and debate associated with the TASK programme is the wide and divergent 'stakeholders' involved with sustainable development in Wales. From government to business to voluntary and community groups and from schoolchildren to committed enthusiasts to sceptical businessmen and women, sustainable development is in the words of Morgan and Morley (Chapter 3), "a collective social endeavour". A consequence of this is that if sustainable development is to be implemented effectively in Wales, a structured way of making things happen on the ground is required that involves communities and volunteers in decision making, and provides a process and context that will allow sustainable development to become a social process which engages people at all levels. This is quite a different model to that so far implemented by the Welsh Assembly Government that emphasises government actions and commitments rather than a 'bottom up' movement.

The challenging suggestion made by a number of authors is that sustainable development requires a fundamentally different view of areas of policy and activity that have previously been regarded as rather mundane or unexciting, such as waste or school meals. Dealing imaginatively and seriously with issues such as these at the regional level will demonstrate a political commitment to sustainable development and avoid a situation where it is seen as a somewhat cynical 'add-on' and not a fundamental part of political or organisational strategy. Cohen (Chapter 5) highlights areas where the lack of 'joined-up thinking' hinders progress in waste management and policy delivery.

Alongside this level of commitment and 'political adventure', there seem to be some fundamental problems – not only visible at a regional level but also at a national and global level – with the meaning and scope of sustainable development. As noted in the introductory chapter of this book, the TASK projects found that many stakeholders in Wales have differing and often conflicting views about the meaning of sustainable development and accepted a broad description of the scope of sustainable development rather than focus on definitions in order for progress to be made. If the researchers working on TASK projects encountered problems, is it likely that use of the term 'sustainable development' will lead to significant difficulties in taking action in the region. As Peattie sets out (Chapter 6), "What needs to be communicated to people is a coherent vision of sustainable development as a whole so that they become familiar with the interconnection of the three "dimensions"; so that when one is visible, there is still awareness of the connection to the other two".

Leadership & education of leaders

The leadership of the sustainable development agenda for Wales is clearly in the hands of the National Assembly and its politicians and policy makers. As described above, this will almost certainly be the case in any regional governance context given the importance of the regional level of government in setting the policies, advancing the implementation and, in some cases, passing the required legislation for sustainable development in the region. However, leadership is not simply a question of gaining elected office and in the area of sustainable development the challenge to leaders to perform their roles in this most complex and all pervasive area is very strong. For example, as Flynn and Morgan (Chapter 2) point out there is still confusion about what sustainable development actually is and this needs to be addressed by strong leadership from the centre.

As in many areas of public policy, effective implementation of policy requires leadership from senior figures, both at political and administrative levels. Alongside this leadership a champion (or champions) needs to emerge in order to act as a focus for the policy responses required by sustainable development. The OSKaR research and debates suggest strongly that there is currently no-one at the political or administrative level in Wales championing, as a personal commitment, sustainable development and this weakens the message and causes scepticism amongst the population at large.

The same seems to be the case at the institutional level in Wales. Although the Welsh Assembly Government through the Sustainable Development Scheme has set 'out its stall' quite clearly in respect of sustainable development across government and the Assembly policy environment, the institution itself is not widely seen as a champion of policy implementation. This conclusion must be set alongside the problems faced by the local authorities described to the OSKaR researchers and at the OSKaR debates. At these levels of governance in the region, implementation and championing of sustainable development is said to be left to individuals, sometimes far down the hierarchy of policy responsibility, rather than accepted as a leadership and exemplar role by the political and administrative leaders of the authorities.

The role of Welsh Unitary Authorities is crucial since most observers recognise that the National Assembly for Wales is not able to deliver a sustainable development agenda for the region but, as noted earlier, relies on the local authorities and others to deliver. Unfortunately, as those attending the OSKaR debates reported the position of the local authorities is poorly understood by the Welsh Assembly Government, particularly in respect of waste and procurement. The trust that is therefore required between multi-level governance layers may not be present., Flynn and Morgan (Chapter 2) refer to the "shallow network" that existed between Assembly officials and local authority officers during the development of the Sustainable Development Scheme, contrasting this with the complex network reliant on trust that existed with various groupings represented on the "Glamorgan Group" during the same period. Local authorities do not feel that the issues that they face in implementing sustainable development are understood or taken seriously while regional government continues to make and promote policies and targets for sustainable development that cannot be delivered within existing arrangements.

A further concern with regard to trust is the extent to which sustainable development decisions, monitoring and evaluations can be based on robust, regional level data. The TASK projects, including the WDA Future Technologies project and the University of Wales Bangor's SCEnE project, identified that the ownership, consistency and control of data and information regarding Wales-level and local-level sustainable development impacts to be deficient for the purposes of measuring sustainable development in Wales. The Welsh Assembly Government should certainly consider the need for high level, relevant information and data on sustainable development in Wales to allow progress to be monitored, audited and reported transparently and frequently.

Leadership in sustainable development therefore takes the dimension where the regional government, in the case under discussion the Welsh Assembly Government, is required to lead by example and, as Flynn and Morgan (Chapter 2) indicate, exemplars of best practice need to be promoted. It may even be feasible to establish an independent (from the Welsh Assembly Government) resource that will be able to monitor the implementation of sustainable development in Wales, research and distribute examples of good practice wherever it can be found and to set more ambitious but meaningful targets for the achievement of sustainable development in Wales.

A final feature of leadership in sustainable development that is evident from the OSKaR research is that educating and raising the awareness of sustainable development is a prerequisite of successful leadership and championing of the implementation of sustainable development. Understanding that sustainable development impacts on a broad range of policy areas and that there are limitations to the ability of regional or local government to effect change without the "collective social endeavour" is essential. This understanding and awareness needs to be engendered in the general public but, possibly more importantly, in politicians and administrators in the public services as well as in upper management levels in the private sector. Sustainable development leadership training needs to become a common professional development element across Wales to ensure the commitment and 'buy-in' of senior officials in public sector bodies and our leading companies. Peattie (Chapter 6) establishes that education in sustainable development needs to become mandatory in teacher training, but goes further to suggest that it could also be made a part of training for school governors. The exemplar effect of a demonstrable commitment to and understanding of sustainable development may be the most important action that today's leaders can make for the future of sustainable development policy in Wales.

Structures – partnerships/networks

As noted earlier, it is clear that the regional government cannot effectively implement sustainable development without a strong and sustained commitment from a range of bodies, individuals and networks operating 'on the ground'. These will include voluntary and community groups and special interest groups such as Local Agenda 21. These efforts in favour of sustainable development, external to the Welsh Assembly Government, need to be legitimised and given explicit recognition as part of the sustainable development effort and fabric in Wales. For example, although the Assembly Sponsored Public Bodies in Wales (ASPBs) have a sustainable development duty in their remit letters, Morgan and Morley (Chapter 3) point out that local authorities are constrained by a number of policy and legislative mechanisms. Peattie (Chapter 6) similarly notes that at present sustainable development education in schools is not required to be included within the strategic plan of the Local Education Authorities and therefore does not appear in the development plans of the individual schools.

This makes the role of local authorities in respect of sustainable development a matter for local political choice rather than a matter of leadership and regional government recognition, at least outside the regulatory requirements that affect the local authorities. Bringing these crucial implementation bodies 'inside the camp' will, it is argued, give greater impact and consistency in the development of effective sustainable development implementation measures. As things stand, the OSKaR research suggests that the large public sector organisations, including the local authorities, WDA, Higher education etc, are not setting a good example and it it seems clear that local authorities frequently have new, sustainable development related duties imposed upon them without the resource implications being fully recognised. This causes a dissatisfaction and disenchantment with sustainable development amongst local authorities and citizens at a local level. Structures, networks and partnerships are needed to encourage and increase awareness of sustainable development across Wales and to join local initiatives together to allow them to work co-operatively. Cohen (Chapter 5) highlights the need for a more focused marketing strategy amid the lack of a genuinely Welsh environmental awareness-raising campaign.

Sustainable Development and education

In Chapter 6, Peattie asserts that progress on sustainable development in a region will only be made if "the wider population knows what sustainable development is, and understand why it is worth pursuing." The OSKaR debates revealed a very strong feeling amongst participants that integration of sustainable development into the mainstream of life and policy will take a generation and even then it will only come about through increased awareness and better education. The role of education for sustainable development is therefore crucial and is one reason why an entire chapter of this book is dedicated to research on the topic.

Peattie (Chapter 6) points out that in the absence of better knowledge and understanding about sustainable development, people will be unable to play their roles in a number of areas of civic life, as consumers, voters, investors, managers, workers, parents and citizens. The types of changes and trends identified by Rhisiart (Chapter 7) will seem to overwhelm them because their terms of reference will not adequately allow them to understand the options that face them and their communities in an increasingly unsustainable world. As Peattie summarises: "They will be left neither able to accept the changes that will be required, nor able to contribute effectively to making planned changes become a reality."

Unfortunately education for sustainable development is not as simple or straightforward as it may first appear. This is because the education process itself is complex given the various roles that we all accept at various times and in various places. Peattie (Chapter 6) summarises these as citizens, workers and learners and suggests that the range of tools and approaches that must be engaged in education for sustainable development are equally complex and even more numerous. Alongside this it is clear from the OSKaR research that the teaching resources that are now available to schools and colleges influence the delivery of sustainable development education. Teachers and pupils are also able to access sustainability-related information resources via the Internet and the number of providers of those resources, and the variety of the messages being promoted has grown significantly, however the trust that is required in order to support sustainable development education becomes even more necessary but potentially increasingly elusive.

A further issue raised by the OSKaR debates and supported strongly by Peattie's research is that the approach to sustainability changes as children progress through the educational system. OSKaR debate participants, for example, thought that as far as possible education about, and for, sustainable development should be more broadly based. Specialisation from too early an age was felt to create individuals with too little knowledge and appreciation of other subjects. Peattie (Chapter 6) observes that as a person progresses through the education system sustainability issues "dissipate rather than intensify".

Practical considerations are also revealed in this area of research. For example, the demands on the teacher training courses are considerable and the training for the teaching of sustainable development can be perceived as just one of several new demands. Similarly, the demands made within the curriculum in terms of time and resources means that sustainable development may get ghettoised into smaller and smaller areas of the classroom time and the school grounds themselves. As Peattie reports, if students are taught about the importance of sustainable development principles in a classroom, but then witness these principles being ignored or contradicted in the way the rest of the school operates, the lesson about sustainability is unlikely to heeded or learned. Peattie concludes that sustainable development poses a challenge in all aspects of school management and life.

The wider education challenge seems to be to ensure that sustainable development cannot be dealt with as an additional discipline but to mainstream it into the education process from teacher training to teaching resources to school management to school governor training in order to set the appropriate example for those on the receiving end of formal education.

The vocational challenge is more complex again largely because of the difficulty of persuading companies to undertake sustainable development training when their own commitment to sustainable development practices are not as good as they should be. This again requires a long term commitment and a balance of persuasion and exhortation with compulsion in key areas. For the formal education system Peattie (Chapter 6) concludes that many stakeholders feel that policy makers will need to go further in terms of "investment in ESD, statutory provision for ESD in planning and inspection, and in coordinating many different elements of policy to reinforce the ESD message". If this is the case for formal education it seems even more the case for informal and vocational education and training.

Procurement policy

It is probably in the area of public sector purchasing of goods and services that the 'on the ground' implementation of sustainable development is seen most directly by citizens as well as by business. The public sector in their purchasing and procurement actions can have a significant effect and lead the way to a positive change in the culture and behaviour of the region's population and businesses by approaching procurement as a sustainable development process where the value obtained from the expenditure of public money is viewed as a sustainable development value as well as a monetary value. The evidence from the research chapters dealing with food and construction provides strong messages in this respect. For example, the procurement of construction services can achieve good sustainable development outcomes if there are stable, long-term supply chain partnerships. Involvement in such a partnership, will, it is argued, allow construction companies to deliver a high quality construction service efficiently to time and cost, and provide environmental and wider sustainable development benefits. In the case of the procurement of food for school meals, local authorities are at present forced to operate as if they were private businesses and ignore wider sustainable development related objectives including those of meeting basic standards of nutrition and promoting healthy eating. The procurement culture that is currently dominant needs to change from lowest price to one that values sustainable development outcomes if the implementation of sustainable development at a regional level is to be achieved.

Unfortunately, public services have been widely and repeatedly subjected to unrealistic competitive pressures as a matter of policy at the EU, national, regional and local levels of government. These have forced them to act as if they were private enterprises but without taking account of the sort of requirement to demonstrate corporate social responsibility in the way that private corporations are now required to do. In particular, the prevailing Audit Commission 'mindset' that requires the public sector to select the lowest tender and a narrowly defined 'Best Value' purchasing outcome needs to be modified by more partnering with suppliers in the procurement process, allowing public sector procurement to incorporate sustainable development standards in the evaluation of suppliers of goods and services.

At the same time public sector organisations themselves need to be more creative and confident, particularly in testing the flexibility of the current procurement regulations and practices as Morgan and Morley (Chapter 3) demonstrate from their review of procurement practices in Italy. The OSKaR research identified the opportunity that exists, with the appropriate leadership, for local authorities to lead by example in this area and introduce integrated working between different departments, sustainable development-friendly procurement policies and to consider the life cycle and ecological 'footprint' of the goods and services that they purchase. At the level of the ASPBs, it is worth noting that the Welsh Development Agency has taken a strong lead in this respect and has developed new construction procurement standards and procedures that place a premium on sustainable development support services.

If this change in procurement practice could be achieved it should not be forgotten that businesses that currently supply goods and services would be required to adjust their assumptions significantly about what is required in order for them to win business from the public sector. A sustainable development procurement education process will need to be developed to assist companies to understand, adopt and then exceed new sustainable development principles, practices and procurement criteria.

At the same time as recognising that businesses will need support to deal with a culture change in procurement by public bodies, it should be noted that the additional burden placed particularly on local authorities to make the necessary changes, at least initially, could be considerable. The regional government, in the case of Wales, the Welsh Assembly Government, will need to make provision and provide additional 'transitional' resources if the sustainable development agenda is to be implemented in this important area of policy.

Valuing and funding sustainable development

A fundamental problem with implementing sustainable development at the regional level relates to the considerable extent to which the public sector generally – and local authorities in particular – are subjected regularly and systematically to reviews of the value that they are achieving with their stewardship of public funds. Unfortunately the conventional methods of valuation do not generally recognise the desirable sustainable development outcomes that should be valued. The OSKaR research identified that for the public and private sectors, effective, relevant costing and valuation methods need to be developed for sustainable development. In particular there is a need to internalise certain external costs and allow a true assessment to be made of the real costs of failing to act sustainably. Crucially, the government accounting system does not easily allow local authorities to try this approach although it does seem to be possible, at least in theory, to make the case for using sustainable development criteria. The OSKaR research suggests however, that the current 'Best value' criteria and approach can hinder rather than help efforts to secure sustainable development outcomes from public expenditures by public bodies. For example in the schools meals research (Chapter 3), Best Value is revealed to have decreased the sustainability dimension of in-house school meal provision in Carmarthenshire. Similarly in sustainable development education (Chapter 6) it was noted that although stakeholders believed that the Assembly Government did take sustainable development in education seriously, there were concerns that in implementation the subject will suffer the "value-action gap. This is a fundamental contradiction in public policy that will need to be corrected if sustainable development is to be implemented at a regional level.

If the situation with valuation and incentives is difficult for the public sector itself, the opportunities for real community and voluntary sustainable development activity are made extremely difficult by a sustainable development funding system that, in the experience of many of the contributors to the OSKaR research, is in itself a contradiction to sustainable development. For example the lack of consistent core funding for sustainable development activities means that investment in new activities may be wasted as the subsequent funding round is required to support only 'additional' activities but leaving 'core' activities to dwindle and, often, die. At the same time, funding sources are generally small in size but large in number so that obtaining funding from one source is difficult and substantial amounts of money are spent 'going round in circles'. In order to establish trust and transparency a 'showcase' funding scheme is probably needed, led by a recognisable sustainable development champion – a business figure or very senior politician. It is only in this very high profile and public way that the commitment to embed sustainable development and the long term changes necessary for its implementation can be demonstrated.

Providing data, information & analysis for sustainable development

A common theme in much of the TASK research and activity has been the challenges faced by researchers and policy makers in obtaining, handling and 'owning' the complex data and information required by the complexity of a sustainable development policy and implementation at the regional level. For example, one of the OSKaR research projects undertaken by Cardiff Business School has been engaged in constructing an environmental Input-Output model of Wales. The data gathering and interpretation that this has required has been a significant investment and an impressive achievement. Similarly, one of the main TASK projects, LANDMAP+, has spent considerable time and effort in specifying, gathering and then validating local data for its purposes. Unfortunately, the data and information required is simply not available in most respects. This problem is not confined to specialist statistical data. Other TASK projects, Future Technologies and SCEnE, have also encountered problems in this respect with their own more general data requirements. Sustainable development indicators, or even their raw data sources, are not generally available at the Wales level.

The policy lesson to be derived from these experiences is, on one level, simple; additional and significant effort is required if the statistics, data and other information required for the measurement, monitoring and evaluation of sustainable development at the regional level is to be provided for policy makers. There is however another level of policy lesson to be drawn here. This is related to the trust that is required to allow for policy makers and politicians to make key decisions that affect the economy, society and the cultural, environmental and spatial development of the region. Sustainable development policy choices are, on the one hand, 'big' decisions affecting the environment etc but they are also very local decisions regarding the landscape, the provision of basic services and needs of society. Sustainable development decision-making therefore requires data and evidence that the general population can trust for its accuracy and lack of bias.

For example, as the Sustainable Futures chapter strongly indicates (Chapter 7), in the coming decades there will be a significantly greater need for local data about changing trends affecting the community, not simply the region. At the same time, the integrated datasets required to make planning decisions related to a broad range of sustainable development factors, as demonstrated by LANDMAP+, are currently not readily available. Similarly, if informed decisions about the future technology opportunities and needs of the region are to be made, region specific data and information is needed but, as the Future Technologies project has shown, this does not currently exist. Finally, as the SCEnE project suggests, the best way to encourage and stimulate small companies and communities to take sustainable development seriously may be to construct benchmark datasets of the region, its companies and communities to allow them to know if they are doing well in comparison to their competitors and peers.

Finding a way of providing, validating and making such data and information transparently available to all of Wales and its stakeholders would be a major step forward for the National Assembly's Sustainable Development policy.

Sustainable futures

The experience of the TASK projects is that there is a need for better, more direct and more consistent dialogues between key stakeholders in the region including scientists, industrial leaders, policy makers and the public. A strong commitment to a consistent programme of futures work involving research – and dialogue and structured discussion – is needed particularly since, as a sample survey conducted by Cardiff Business School in the Royal Welsh Show, National Eisteddfod and Urdd Eisteddfod over the summer of 2003 found, the public is sceptical about the extent to which scientists, politicians and business can be trusted with the future.

The scenarios presented in the futures chapter present policy-makers and society as a whole with challenges and fundamental choices. At a regional level, governments do have some scope to influence the trends and create for the region and its people a sustainable future. However, a commitment to a sustained process of scenario building and analysis is needed if these sustainable futures are to have any chance of being realised.

Chapter 9

Conclusion

Meirion Thomas and Martin Rhisiart

I f the statutory commitment of the National Assembly for Wales to promote sustainable development in Wales is to be achieved all of Welsh society and economy needs to become engaged. In particular, the "political adventure" and "collective social endeavour" that the Assembly's commitment to sustainable development represents requires the information, research and understanding that will allow Wales, and Welsh based institutions, to implement sustainable development effectively and efficiently.

As a number of the contributors to this book assert, the regional level is where sustainable development is most obviously implemented. This gives the regions of Europe a particularly striking responsibility if the regions wish to shape their own sustainable futures rather than relying on policy prescriptions handed down from the global, supra-national or national levels of governance. Therefore while it is greatly encouraging that the European Union has challenged regions to find the solutions and policy prescriptions for sustainable development that are appropriate for Europe's regions, it is vital for Wales, Welsh researchers and those engaged in civic debate to make practical, well researched and informed contributions to the sustainable development debate. Sustainable development is an increasingly important area of study at an academic but also at a practical policy and implementation level. This book and the different perspectives that it has explored will, we hope, make its own important and thought provoking contribution to finding those appropriate solutions and policy prescriptions for regions.

The material reported in this book is the result of the research, debate and discussion that has taken place over a two-year period led by the Cardiff Business School and supported by the European Union's Innovative Actions programme and the Welsh Assembly Government. It has helped to create a regional "laboratory" to test new approaches to sustainable development at the regional level. Cardiff Business School is grateful for the financial support and the wide access that these governmental bodies operating at very different but highly engaged governance levels have afforded the authors.

Obviously, the book and the research which stimulated it has taken a Welsh focus but the findings of the research and the policy lessons derived from the research and the whole OSKaR exercise are, we believe, widely applicable at a regional level across the EU and globally. The lessons learned in the initial stages of implementing sustainable development at a regional governance level are certainly widely applicable while the sector focus of the research studies contained in the book were chosen specifically because they are applicable in many regions, countries and circumstances. Indeed the emphasis throughout the OSKaR research has been on learning the policy lessons emanating from the experience of implementing the sustainable development agenda in Wales but set against a 'benchmark' of other European regional experiences of sustainable development implementation. We hope that the resulting research results and perspectives are, consequently, of wide practical and theoretical relevance.

The policy lessons drawn from the research featured in this book and elsewhere from the OSKaR project cover areas where action can be taken by government, NGOs and in a number of cases, by individuals. For example, taking action in the policy governance framework to ensure continued collaboration and consultation is clearly on the National Assembly agenda for the future. Although some of the lessons drawn here may appear to be critical of the Assembly, they should be read in the context and understanding that they can only be made because of the Assembly's openness and commitment to implementing the sustainable development agenda across the whole of Welsh society and economy. Similarly, the need for more visible and sustained leadership - and the education of the leaders throughout society - is an essential policy lesson drawn in this book and the book itself is intended as an input to that education and awareness raising.

In a number of areas, the policy lessons relate to highly practical actions that are required, for example in terms of public procurement in the areas of food, construction and waste. Also in this category are the changes in the 'valuation' of outputs from public policy and associated expenditures that are necessary to ensure that sustainable development is adequately reflected in the assessment of those policy outcomes.

The future is, as ever, uncertain. Achieving a sustainable future for Wales, as a region and country where sustainable development is at the top of society's agenda as well as the top of the political agenda, will be challenging. The policy lessons of this book suggest that continued efforts must be made to develop a clear understanding of the development options and trajectories that are open for Wales in achieving its sustainable development objective. The future development of the sustainable development agenda in Wales (and in any region) relies to a very significant extent on trust that politicians, policy makers and business leaders can create and maintain amongst the general public. This trust must be extended to policy commitments, reliability of information and the commitments to resourcing the implementation steps necessary for the achievement of a Sustainable Region.

We hope that this book will encourage mutual understanding and debate of the issues so that Sustainable Development can indeed work in regional economies.